Out of the Wilderness

American University Studies

Series VII
Theology and Religion
Vol. 51

PETER LANG
New York • Bern • Frankfurt am Main • Paris

Preston Warren

Out of the Wilderness

Douglas Clyde Macintosh's
Journeys Through the Grounds
and Claims of Modern Thought

PETER LANG
New York • Bern • Frankfurt am Main • Paris

Library of Congress Cataloging-in-Publication Data

Warren, Preston
   Out of the wilderness.

   (American university studies. Series VII, Theology and religion ; vol. 51)
     Bibliography: p.
     Includes index.
     1. Macintosh, Douglas Clyde, 1877-1948.
2. Theologians — United States — Biography. I. Title.
II. Series.
BX4827.M24W37   1989   230'.6'0924 [B]   88-9475
ISBN 0-8204-0777-1
ISSN 0740-0446

CIP–Titelaufnahme der Deutschen Bibliothek

Warren, Preston:
Out of the wilderness : Douglas Clyde Macintosh's Journeys through the grounds and claims of modern thought / Preston Warren. – New York; Bern; Frankfurt am Main; Paris: Lang, 1988.
   (American University Studies: Ser. 7, Theology and Religion; Vol. 51)
   ISBN 0-8204-0777-1

NE: American University Studies / 07

© Peter Lang Publishing, Inc., New York 1989

All rights reserved.
Reprint or reproduction, even partially, in all forms such as microfilm, xerography, microfiche, microcard, offset strictly prohibited.

Printed by Weihert-Druck GmbH, Darmstadt, West Germany

Portrait of Douglas Macintosh

TO: Alce
    Rollin
    Lynne
    Carolyn

DOUGLAS CLYDE MACINTOSH

TABLE OF CONTENTS

FOREWARD xi
ABBREVIATIONS xiii
ACKNOWLEDGEMENTS xv
PREFACES:
  1: AMERICAN CITIZENSHIP: A MIRAGE 1
  2: FACETS OF THE MAN 13

CHAPTER I: BIOGRAPHICALLY, DOUGLAS CLYDE MACINTOSH . . 29
CHAPTER II: THE PILGRIM'S PROCESS 41
CHAPTER III: SOME PILGRIM'S VISIONS 55
CHAPTER IV: RECOURSE TO PRAGMATICS 69
CHAPTER V: BEING REALISTIC 81
CHAPTER VI: RELIGIOUS REALISM 95
CHAPTER VII: A CRITICAL REALIST'S DIVINITY 121
CHAPTER VIII: VALUATIONAL AND SOCIAL REALISMS 135
CHAPTER IX: RESPONSES TO CRITICS 161
CHAPTER X: THE MACINTOSH BEQUEST 191

APPENDIX 219
PUBLICATIONS OF DOUGLAS C. MACINTOSH 225
FOOTNOTES 239
INDEX 265

FOREWARD

Professor Warren died in June this year (1988). He had completed every part and aspect of his manuscript except the comprehensive bibliography. In poor health for years he resolutely and cheerfully devoted his diminishing energy to completing this splendid study of Macintosh. Professor Warren was eminently qualified for this enterprise. The result is the definitive account of Douglas Clyde Macintosh, a great teacher and an important figure in American religious thought. Professor Warren's family and friends deeply regret that it was not given to him to see the finished product.

Julian Noris Hartt
July 1988

Index to Abbreviations

C A T	--	Contemporary American Theology
C N	--	Class Notes
D C M	--	Douglas Clyde Macintosh
D C M F	--	Douglas Clyde Macintosh Fellowship
P R	--	The Pilgrimage of Faith in the World of Modern Thought
P K	--	The Problem of Knowledge
P R	--	Personal Religion
P R K	--	The Problem of Religious Knowledge
P R R	--	The Philosophy of Physical Realism
R C	--	The Reasonableness of Christianity
R R	--	Religious Realism
S R	--	Social Religion

ACKNOWLEDGEMENTS

While employing a considerable number of sources, I find that I need permission for quoting from only one of these. Tabulation from my footnotes shows that I have used nineteen diverse sources of Macintosh's own writings. Those employed most extensively include:

<blockquote>

The Problem of Knowledge, Macmillan Co., 1915

Religious Realism, Macmillan Co., 1931

The Pilgrimage of Faith in the World of Modern Thought, University of Calcutta Press, 1931

Contemporary Theology, Vol. I, 1932

Review of Religion, 3 issues in 1939 and 1940

Social Religion, Scribners Sons, 1939

The Problem of Religious Knowledge, Harper, 1940.

</blockquote>

All of these sources are now in the public domain but I am no less indebted to the publishers and have, accordingly, acknowledged them in my footnotes. The Beacon Press, to which I wrote for permission to quote from Roy Wood Sellars' essay, "Accept the Universe as a Going Concern," in Religious Liberals Reply (1947), responded that that volume was likewise in the public domain and otherwise acceptable, with, of course, proper footnoting.

The one later volume quoted rather extensively, is a symposium edited by Bernard E. Meland on The Future of Empirical Theology, (University of Chicago Press, 1969). A most courteous letter from the Permissions Editor of the Press has informed me that my quotations from four authors in the volume, "most certainly fall into the category of 'fair use'" and that therefore it is my judgment that "no formal permission is necessary." I am deeply gratified that I can, thereby, relate Macintosh to significant confluences of later theological thought.

I have also had the benefits of Randolph Crump Miller's The American Spirit in Theology, (United Church Press, 1974), but have found it easier to paraphrase and, thereby, to desist from exact quotation. Miller, in fact, has been my chief recent consultant. His endorsements of my comprehensions of Douglas Macintosh's theology and philosophy of religion, and suggestion of a section on the enduring values of Macintosh have kept this mid-octogenarian kindled for the completion of his efforts.

Besides Yale's Professor Randolph Miller I must include two other readers in my Acknowledgements. Former Yale Professor Julian Hartt was my first reader and he is assisting me basically now. Bucknell's Professor Harry Garvin (former Editor of the Bucknell Review) read my first five chapters, making basic editorial suggestions.

My three typists must not be omitted. Iva Weaver was the first of these and Sally Stewart the second. She is now combining my own professional typing with her full-time work. Deborah Lecuyer has become my typist for the final copy of this manuscript. My indebtedness to each is quite substantial.

I would gladly also cite the contributors to my considerable overhead but individual credits would require listing three of my siblings along with other relatives and concerned friends.

PREFACE 1

AMERICAN CITIZENSHIP: A MIRAGE

Canadian-born Douglas Clyde Macintosh, whose centennial was celebrated at Yale in 1977 and new portrait unveiled in 1980, was most generally known from the publicity given to his efforts to obtain U.S. citizenship. That this was a variously misunderstood episode in his life calls for an elaboration of the nature and motivations of that life, and, first of all, for a succinct review of his attempts to become an official U.S. citizen. As a theologian and an exponent of the philosophy of religion, he would wish to gain citizenship as early as possible. And that is just what he set about to do. Why then all the "to do"? The story has its fascinations.

His very first attempt to enter the USA officially was attended with two anomalous circumstances. He had been a student for a doctorate of philosophy at the University of Chicago. Going back and forth between Canada and the U.S. had been easy on a temporary basis. But when in 1909 he proceeded to enter America to become Assistant Professor of Systematic Theology at Yale University, residential problems immediately emerged. Asked by an immigration officer on his train where he was going and whether he had a job awaiting him in New Haven, Connecticut, taciturn Macintosh simply replied in the affirmative. "Where were you when this contract was made," asked the officer. "Canada," answered Macintosh. "You will have to get off the train. You cannot enter the United States," asserted the officer. "But," said Macintosh, "the President of the United

States is on the corporation that is employing me." "What are you going to do in New Haven?" asked the officer. "I am going to be a professor at Yale University" was the reply. "Oh," said the officer, "that is all right. I thought you said you were coming over to work."[1]

But when Macintosh, in due course, proceeded to prepare his application for citizenship, he was told that there was no record of his entry into the country, and that he was not officially a resident. So, returning from a summer visit in Ontario, he took care to make another official entry. Attempting a second time to apply for citizenship, he was again told that there was no record of his residence. He made a trip to the Bureau of Naturalization in Washington to explain his admission and presence in Connecticut. "That doesn't matter," they informed him.

So he made a third effort to obtain residential status. But before he could apply for citizenship this time, his native land was at war with Germany, and he obtained a leave-of-absence to go overseas as a chaplain with the Canadian army. A tribute to his service as chaplain came to me from a professor of mine, Lt. Colonel J.H. MacDonald, who had been a senior chaplain in World War I. He related that when Macintosh was leaving his unit to transfer to the U.S. Army, following the entry of the United States into World War I, he was given a flask inscribed by all the officers of his company.

It was 1929 before Macintosh was actually able to file an application for citizenship, twenty years after his appointment to the Yale faculty. Macintosh was then 52. And by then there was a questionnaire to be answered, to protect the country from saboteurs and undesirables. Question #22 read: "If necessary, are you willing to bear arms in defense of this country?" Macintosh was no ultra-pacifist, <u>as his own war record showed</u>, and at 52 the question was largely academic. But it was academic in a special sense. He was a spokesman for the Christian conscience. Hence his response was "Yes, but I should like to be free to judge of the necessity." In trying to explain this to the Naturalization Examiner and to Judge Burrows before whom he appeared in the Federal District Court in New Haven, he said,

> "I could not take the prescribed oath of allegiance without intepreting it, of course, and if allowed to interpret it for myself, I would interpret it as not in conflict with my position, and would take it in good faith. If, however, the examiner of the judge were to do the interpreting, I must accept that interpretation and decide accordingly. I had never taken the position of absolute pacifism, because I could not be sure that never under any possible circumstances would a defensive or police use of military force be justified; on the other hand, I was still surer that it would not be right for me to give a blanket promise beforehand that I would support any and every war in which the future Government of my country might engage.* It would be hard enough at the time

---

*Not all good American citizens have supported all wars in which the United States has engaged in the past: <u>Daniel Webster, Charles Sumner</u>, and <u>Abraham Lincoln opposed and denounced the Mexican War as morally unjustified; and Grover Cleveland and Benjamin Harrison took a similar attitude toward the war with Spain</u>."

to know that a war was morally justified; it was quite impossible to know that a future war would be morally justified when one had as yet no idea as to what it would be about. I did not subscribe to the type of patriotism involved in the slogan, 'My country, right or wrong!' True patriotism, as I understood it, would recognize special obligation to one's own country, but it would not consider it the duty of a citizen to seek the apparent well-being of his own country by a course obviously opposed to the welfare of the world in the long run. I was ready to give the United States, in return for citizenship, all the allegiance I had ever given or could ever give to any country. Interpreting the will of God, however, as what is right and for the highest well-being of all humanity, I felt that I ought not to put my allegiance to any country, even my own, above my allegiance to the will of God, thus interpreted. I recognized the principle of the submission of the individual citizen to the opinion of the majority in political matters in a democratic country; but I did not believe in having my own moral opinions settled by the majority. I admitted the right, in general, of the Government to restrain the freedom of the individual for the good of the social whole, but I was convinced that the individual should have the right to withhold his military services (involving the taking of human life) whenever his best moral judgment led him to do so. I felt that it would be only fair, as well as in accord with the Constitution and laws of the United States, if I were to be allowed to become a naturalized citizen on the same free ethical basis as that enjoyed by the native-born citizen. In other words, <u>just as the native-born citizen is a citizen without having had to promise beforehand that he will support any and every war which any future Government of the country may engage in during his lifetime, so, it seemed to me, the naturalized citizen should be a citizen who has not been required to make any immoral promise to do what might possibly seem wrong to him when the time came.</u>"2

The judgment of the Court, however, was as follows:

> "It appearing that the said petitioner, considering his allegiance to be first in the will of God, would not promise in advance to bear arms in defense of the United States under all circumstances, but only if he believed the war to be morally justified, it is:
>
> "Decreed that the petitioner is not attached to the principles of the Constitution of the United States, and further decreed that said petition for citizenship is denied."

Macintosh explains Judge Burrows' probable position in these words, that to admit the "right of a citizen to support only such wars as he could conscientiously regard as morally justified would be dangerous," and he quotes a ministerial friend who put the matter in this paradoxical statement: "If I had been in Judge Burrows' place, I should have done as he did." Other (legal) minds, we shall find, did not treat the Judge's position as inescapable. The New York Herald Tribune, to be sure, gave him an endorsement on the grounds that to make one's own conscience the final arbiter of his conduct was "nothing more or less than a challenge of the whole Anglo-Saxon principle of majority rule." To this the editor of the New York World, in turn, asked: "Has it occurred to the Herald Tribune that its position is nothing more nor less than a challenge to the principle of moral responsibility?"[3]

Sharp divisions of opinion were rife. Yale University was actually attacked by a veterans' organization from a nearby town for continuing to keep Macintosh on its faculty, though at least one member of that group came to Macintosh prepared to offer an affidavit that while so "patriotically" attacking Macintosh's conscience, the organization was itself engaged in illegal and, hence, disloyal activities.

It should be mentioned that this was a time of extreme pacifisms, as well as one in which alien prostitutes and underworld "businessmen" were gaining, or attempting to gain access, to the United States. This set of circumstances provided a background against which the fever engendered by the Macintosh case was accentuated. Most undesirable applicants, however, would have little difficulty answering question #22. They could readily agree to defend the country and then proceed to undermine it.

Among Macintosh's active supporters was Jerome Davis, Associate Professor of Social Ethics at Yale Divinity School. He urged his legal friend, Allen Wardwell, to carry the case to the U.S. Appellate Court. Wardwell, in turn, recommended to his distinguished partner, John W. Davis, that they do this without fee. The case was argued before Judges Manton, Swann, and Learned Hand who <u>unanimously</u> reversed the decision of Judge Burrows. The reversing opinion was explained by Judge Manton as follows:

> "It appears that the applicant stated that he was ready to give to the United States in return for citizenship all the allegiance he had ever given or could give to any Country, but that he could not put allegiance to the government of any country before allegiance to the will of God. . . . There is a distinction between a morally justified and an unjustifiable war as recognized in international law. Recognition was given to such distinction in the recent Kellogg pact."

Quoting Judge Story's work on the Constitution, where he says,

> "The rights of conscience are, indeed, beyond the just reach of any human power. They are given by God and cannot be encroached upon by human authority, without criminal disobedience of the precepts of natural as well as revealed religion,"

Judge Manton went on to say,

> "The rights of conscience are inalienable rights which the citizen need not surrender and which the government or society cannot take away . . . . No more is demanded of an alien who becomes a citizen than a natural born citizen, and when an alien becomes a citizen he is accorded all the rights and privileges afforded to a natural born citizen except eligibility to the Presidency."[4]

The case, however, was appealed by the Government to the United States Supreme Court. Macintosh's own account of this follows:

> The counsel for the respondent consisted of John W. Davis, Charles E. Clark (Dean of the Yale School of Law), Allen Wardwell, and W. Charles Poletti. The Government's case was presented to the Supreme Court by Solicitor General Thomas D. Thacker. The case for respondent was argued by Mr. Davis, who said, among other things, 'God knows what we want now is not more men who agree with the majority but who are willing to go against the majority on occasion.' On May 25, 1931, the judgment handed down showed a 5-to-4 decision reversing the judgment of the Court of Appeals and denying citizenship to the respondent. The majority was made up of Justices Van Devanter, McReynolds, Sutherland, Butler, and Roberts; the dissenting votes were cast by Chief Justice Hughes and Justices Holmes, Brendeis, and Stone.

In voicing the opinion of the Court, Justice Sutherland took a position very broad in scope, applying his interpretations of the limits imposed upon conscience by Government to the native-born citizen as well as to the naturalized. He said in part:

'Naturalization is a privilege, to be given, qualified or withheld as Congress may determine, and which the alien may claim as of right only upon compliance with the terms which Congress imposes. . . . From its very nature the war power, when necessity calls for its exercise, tolerates no qualifications or limitations, unless found in the Constitution or in applicable principles of international law. . . . Whether any citizen shall be exempt from serving in the armed forces of the Nation in time of war is dependent upon the will of Congress and not upon the scruples of the individual, except as Congress provides. . . . The war powers [of Congress] include . . . the power in the last extremity, to compel the armed service of and citizen in the land, without regard to his objections or his views in respect of the justice or morality of the particular war or of war in general. The applicant . . . is unwilling to become a citizen with this understanding. He is unwilling to leave the question of his future military service to the wisdom of Congress where it belongs, and where every native-born or admitted citizen is obliged to leave it. . . . When he speaks of putting his allegiance to the will of God above his allegiance to the Government, it is evident . . . that he means to make <u>his own interpretation</u> of the will of God the <u>decisive test</u>. . . . We are a Christian people, according to one another the equal right of religious freedom, and acknowledging with reverence the duty of obedience to the will of God. But, also, we are a Nation with the duty to survive; a Nation whose Constitution contemplates war as well as peace; whose government must go forward upon the assumption, and safely can proceed upon no other, that unqualified allegiance to the Nation and submission and obedience to the laws of the land, as well as those made for war as those made for peace, is not inconsistent with the will of God.'

The dissenting opinion of Chief Justice Hughes, Justices Holms, Brandeis, and Stone concurring, contained, among other statements, the following:

> 'The question before the Court is . . . whether Congress has exacted . . . the pomise to bear arms as a condition of its grant of naturalization . . . Congress has not made such an express requirement. . . . I think that the requirement should not be implied, because such a construction is directly opposed to the spirit of our institutions and to the historic practice of the Congress. . . . Departmental zeal may not be permitted to outrun the authority conferred by statute. If such a promise is to be demanded, contrary to principles which have been respected as fundamental, the Congress should enact it in unequivocal terms and we should not, by judicial decision, attempt to perform what, as I see it, is a legislative function.
>
> 'That the general words [of the oath] have not been regarded as implying a promise to bear arms notwithstanding religious or conscientious scruples, or as requiring one to promise to put allegiance to temporal power above what is sincerely believed to be one's duty of obedience to God, is apparent, I think, from a consideration of their history. This oath . . . is the same oath in substances that is required of civil officers generally. . . . When we consider the history of the stuggle for religious liberty, the large number of citizens of our country from the very beginning who have been unwilling to sacrifice their religious convictions, and in particular those who have been conscientiously opposed to war and who would not yield what they sincerely believed to be their allegiance to the will of God, I find it impossible to conclude that such persons are to be deemed disqualified for public office in this country because of the requirement of the oath which must be taken before they enter upon their duties. . . . The requirement of the oath of office should be read in the light of our regard from the beginning for freedom of conscience.

'Much has been said of the paramount
duty to the State, a duty to be recognized,
it is urged, even though it conflicts with
convictions of duty to God. Undoubtedly that
duty to the State exists within the domain of
power, for government may enforce obedience
to laws regardless of scruples. When one's
belief collides with the power of State, the
latter is supreme within its sphere and
submission or punishment follows. But, in
the forum of conscience, duty to a moral
power higher than the State has always been
maintained. . . . The essence of religion is
belief in a relation to God involving duties
superior to those arising from any human
relation. . . . One cannot speak of religious
liberty, with proper appreciation of its
essential and historical significance, without assuming the existence of a belief in
supreme allegiance to the will of God. . . .
There is abundant room for enforcing the
requisite authority of law . . . without
demanding that either citizens or applicants
for citizenship shall assume by oath an
obligation to regard allegiance to God as
subordinate to allegiance to civil power'." [5]

The implications of the Supreme Court decision were soon drawn. It was seen that the decision "affects not only an applicant for naturalization but every native-born American . . . and lends itself to a justification of any form of tyranny over the free conscience of American citizens."[6]

Legislation had, in fact, been introduced by Congressman Anthony Griffin as early as May 1929, to remedy this developing crisis of citizenship. In December 1931, a further bill was offered by Senator Bronson Cutting, and then reintroduced in January 1938, without positive results.

The case of a French Canadian Seventh Day Adventist, James Louis Girouard, brought a turning point on citizenship for conscientious objectors. Stating that he would serve as a non-combatant in war but would not bear arms, he was admitted to citizenship in a U.S. Massachusetts court. The Government secured a reversal on an appeal but in April 1946--seventeen years after Macintosh had filed his application--the Supreme Court reversed the Appellate Court's verdict about Girouard's citizenship and by doing so overturned other decisions including that about Macintosh.[7] Justice Douglas' opinion in this 1946 decision explained that a 1942 Constitutional Amendment gave affirmative recognition that one "could be attached to the principles of government without bearing arms." He added that "freedom of religion guaranteed by the first Amendment is the product of that "long long struggle" of men who have suffered death rather than subordinate their allegiance to God to that of the State.[8]

Macintosh was now an invalid, having suffered a disabling stroke in 1942 (when he was retired as Professor Emeritus). He had, in fact, given up the quest for citizenship following the Supreme Court's decision in 1931.

There was, he said, "a bright side to the picture. I was to have two countries, the land of my birth and the land of my adoption. I can sing 'My country, 'tis of thee,' and mean part of it for Canada and part of it for the United States. These are my two countries, and I love them both. As for what I shall do when these two countries go to war with each other--I will cross that bridge when I come to it! Nothing would please me more than to see the United States and the British Commonwealth of Nations, of which Canada is one, united--not necessarily politically, of course, but united in the strengthening of each other's hands in everything that can be wisely done for peace and freedom and democracy, and in general for the good life, the life of the good neighbor and ultimately of economic and social justice for all."[9]

POSTHUMOUSLY

An attempt in 1980 to obtain honorary posthumous citizenship for Macintosh seemed to be in process of passage. Senator Ribicoff of Connecticut presented a Resolution for such citizenship in the Senate where it had early passage, but the large number of new congressmen at the time of President Reagan's election and new programs kept the Congressional form of the resolution permanently "bottled" in the House Committee. Unofficially, Macintosh remains, in the matter of citizenship, a victim of historic circumstance.

PREFACE 2

FACETS OF THE MAN

We have had one glimpse into the qualities of the man whose quest for citizenship was mishandled by officials, if not by the Courts. I wish now to present other facets of Douglas Macintosh by way of tributes. There have been many of these, most notably on his sixtieth birthday, the centennial of his birth in 1977, and the unveiling of a new portrait of him three years later. I shall start, however, with a letter to me from Julius Seelye Bixler, former Harvard professor and later President of Colby College. Like others I shall cite, Bixler is now deceased. In 1978 he wrote the following in response to an inquiry from me:

> "I first met him in 1922. I had been teaching in Beirut and decided that I must come home and get a Ph.D. . . . I remember making a beeline from the boat to New Haven . . . finding Mac at his office (Edwards Hall) and spending about two hours with him. In his objective and reserved way he was at the same time so kind and considerate, so ready to be confident about the abilities of the person confronting him . . . that he actually gave me just the feeling of assurance I so badly needed while at the same time offering some practical hints. I knew from that moment that he was the one I wanted to work with. I spent that year at Yale, then went to Chicago that next summer partly because Mac was to be there. . . . He was just about the greatest teacher I ever had. . . . [A]s you will remember, his classroom manner was detached, almost aloof. He gave the impression of a rather shy, reserved person. There was no dependence on classroom fireworks or on the 'give and take' which some teachers are able to use very successfully. But to listen to the absorbing clarity of his exposition was to have the feeling of really penetrating to the essence of the subject

in hand. It was though he had presented us with a vision of some of Husserl's essences--objects which had to be so and couldn't be otherwise. 'This is It' we used to say to ourselves as we heard him. Here in all their luminosity were the greatest ideas which we had struggled for so long to see and understand."

"Huxley once wrote to Kingsley (I haven't the exact quotation but this is what I recall): 'Science seems to me to teach in the strongest possible manner the truth of the conception of entire devotion to the will of God. Sit down before fact as a little child, be prepared to give up every preconceived notion, follow humbly wherever and to whatever abyss leads--or you will learn nothing'."

"I think Macintosh gave us this impression of absolutely uncompromising devotion to the truths--of philosophy this time rather than science--and this was one reason why we were so thrilled. He set before us what we knew we ought to want. There was no trimming down to make allowances for us or for any special point of view. But in having our attention fixed on the truly objective, that which was good in itself and in its independence, we found what we ourselves wanted."

". . . what a man for clear definitions! 'Knowledge is adequate certitude of what is really present'. And what a man of faith! There is ultimately a harmony between what is good for man to believe and what is true'."

Bixler was also a participant in the 60th birthday dinner in 1937 honoring Macintosh with a Festschrift. In that connection, however, I shall quote the distinguished Yale Church Historian Roland Bainton, who died in his 90s in 1987. He has paid more than one tribute to Macintosh as we shall have occasion to note. Regarding the testimonial dinner, he tells of "Reinhold Niebuhr's saying that Mac's next book should be entitled, "My Former

Students and Other Battle Lines."[1] This bit of a jibe, however, did not so much reflect sharp debates (in class) as rather, the independence of thought that Macintosh brought out in his students. Yet there could have been something more than jest in Macintosh's reply to Niebuhr's tribute when he said that he was reminded of a "professor of philosophy who when congratulated on the number of his students in distinguished posts replied, 'Yes, and no one of them is teaching the truth'." Niebuhr's own essay in the leather-bound Festschrift on The Nature of Religious Experience presented to Macintosh at this time entitled "The Truth in Myths." And Bixler wrote: "Religion cannot allow its interest to be centered exclusively in the factual world, nor can it forget that the bridge between the world of fact and the world of meaning must take its form from the ideal as well as the real." Yet he also wrote me, "But how strongly he did come back at us in three reviews of the book (Festschrift) in The Review of Religion. Of course Mac could outthink us with one hand tied behind him, and some of his comments on our contributions were devastating."[2]

Professor Julian Hartt, who succeeded Macintosh at Yale, wrote in a Centennial tribute to him in 1977.[3] "In my first year as a graduate student I took his famous year-long seminar in the Theory of Knowledge. On no occasion that year did he ever raise his voice above a soft conversational tone, either to underscore a philosophical point or to reprove dullness or perversity. He listened in apparently inexhaustible patience to things he must have known were ill-considered . . . but the most extreme criticism I think I heard him utter all year was, 'Well, I suppose what you say might be possible.' We all learned that that was the full equivalent, from others, of, 'How can you possibly propose such an absurdity'?"

"At the beginning of my second year," Hartt continued, "Macintosh asked me whether I would like to read papers written by the students in his Systematic Theology . . . Macintosh knew that the Hartts were [then] poor (years before the Gravytrain of graduate school fellowships . . .). He was much too thoughtful a person simply to offer us charity. So he offered me a job instead . . . which he paid for out of his pocket. (Later I was to learn that he subsidized a lot of students one way or another, but never with any advertisement.) "His shipment to Hartt later of a box of copies of all of his writings . . . and all of them autographed was a gesture characteristic of the man."

The "unveiling" of February 13, 1980, brought the reflections of three contemporary professors and of the artist who painted both the original and the new portrait. Explaining why he painted a second picture--without compensation--Clarence Brodeur related that the vandalizing of the first portrait in the 1960s had not gained his attention until recent vigorous efforts by divinity student Paul (Douglas Macintosh) Keane had gained publicity in the New Haven Register. He thereupon offered to replace the portrait. Why did he do so? First, a considerable number of people had contributed to the cost of the original painting. Secondly, Brodeur had been so impressed with Macintosh while painting him in 1946--despite the latter's paralyzing stroke (in 1942)--that he believed such a personage should be perpetuated in art. And, as he restudied the evidence concerning Macintosh, he became convinced that the portrait should not be just a restoration of a paralyzed man but the presentation of a singularly vital person, who was in fact a fighter. The <u>Register</u> had characterized Macintosh as a pacifist of the late twenties and early thirties, but he had served as Chaplain to both Canadian and U.S. Armed Forces in World War I. Yet when he applied for U.S. Citizenship in 1929 [which he had tried to do on two earlier occasions] he had responded to the question, Are you willing to bear arms in defense of the United States of America? as already indicated in the first Preface, that he would be willing to do so in what he rationally believed to be a just war, but that there might be wars in which as a Christian [theologian] he could not participate. An unjust war would not be in accordance with the will of God. The commandment, thou shalt have no other gods before me, was a morally religious principle that could not be conscientiously ignored.

Brodeur's tribute was followed by three others that amplified Macintosh's singular qualities. The first was that of Professor Raymond P. Morris, who had first met Macintosh in 1932, years after the latter had become established as "one of the foremost, if not <u>the</u> important liberal theologian of the time." Thirty years Macintosh's junior, Morris found Macintosh simple, approachable, and distinctive, a man who undertook to encourage his younger colleagues and was strongly supportive of the moral rights of less junior ones, as when the University dismissed

Jerome Davis rather than promote him to a full professorship. Macintosh was well-organized, disciplined, and almost supremely industrious, with an amazing capacity for recall. He was so devoted to students that he made his way to his office for appointments with them in winter weather that closed most offices, and during the Depression he had Morris and others <u>anonymously</u> deposit sizeable sums of money in an account for student assistance. (Sworn to secrecy, Morris divulged this for the first time at this unveiling.) Morris had wrestled, unsuccessfully, with Macintosh's <u>Problem of Knowledge</u>, yet at Beacon's Falls, Connecticut, he had discovered his profoundly impressive simplicity as a spokesman for evangelical religion.

The Yale graduate Professor of Religious Studies, Hans Frei, was the next speaker. He had come to Yale as a student after Macintosh's stroke in 1942, and Macintosh had already been succeeded by his recent graduate student Julian Hartt. Except in Hartt's courses, Macintosh's writings were not being seriously studied--even in courses taught by his former students. These very teachers were indeed exercising the capacities for independent thought which Macintosh had elicited in them. Macintosh's religious philosophy, in consequence, went into a virtual eclipse. It was his spirit that survived rather than his thought, even though the impact of his thought on such former students as Richard Niebuhr was evident in the latter's struggle with the place of value in theology.

Reading Macintosh, moreover, one is in for surprises. His plain straightforward style cradled a strong and very direct religion and seems to report on things as they are: on God as a dependable power that makes for righteousness, an objective factor to which we may adjust rightly or wrongly--and not just a value actor or a ground of Being. His theology has the rigor of a puritanism and yet it expresses, in Jane Austen's phrase, the serenity of a mind at peace with itself, and it takes account of the wide range of theological thought and of discoveries regarding religion. It is not surprising, therefore, that over thirty-three years he had become a virtual by-word at Yale.

Professor of Christian Nuture Randolph C. Miller provided warm personal reminiscenses of Macintosh. Coming from California at 21, he had taken Mac's courses in Systematic Theology, Philosophy of Religion, and the Theory of Knowledge--which was of course, anyway, a real problem even to Macintosh. Macintosh's style was direct, simple, and intellectually challenging. He was, he said, "our favorite professor," and Miller wrote his dissertation under Mac's guidance.

Miller taught at the Church Divinity of the Pacific, where he used Macintosh's <u>Reasonableness of Christianity</u> as a text in his course on Christian Evidences. He had shifted to Religious Education on coming back to Yale and had only two opportunities to teach Mac's Empirical Theology, yet was deeply concerned to memorialize his mentor.

Professor Emeritus Roland Bainton was not in New Haven for the unveiling but had an opportunity to express himself on the third and fourth pages of the program. His theme was that Douglas Macintosh was "one of the giants of the faculty" in his days as a student and junior colleague (Church Historian Walker was another). "As a teacher of Systematic Theology, he [Macintosh] combined three strands which have been woven into the fabric of instruction in this school: pietism, rationalism, and social concern."[4]

We are privileged now to continue with two other tributes from Bainton.

For the first, he reported the heartening that Macintosh gave to his students in the example of "Souren Vetsigian, who has been now for many years in Bulgaria. In 1931 he gave a report which elicited no enthusiasm from a seminar. He was depressed until Macintosh told him that it had the making of an article. That encouragement started him toward the product of several books which have appeared in Armenian."

Bainton continues: "The Professor's concern extended to the wives and children of students also. When the Peter Goertz family, enroute to China, was at the station in Vancouver, B.C., whom should they meet but Douglas Macintosh! While Peter was attending to tickets the Professor sat down with Mrs. Goertz and gave her words of cheer. The Baintons remember him holding their first baby during the cutting of her toenails."[5]

And Bainton reports one of the greatest tributes to Macintosh as a man of special character and concern in the devotion of his wife Hope Conklin Macintosh and her founding of The Douglas Clyde Macintosh Fellowship in Theology and the Philosophy of Religion at Yale. Before elaborating on the Hope Conklin work, however, I should like to relate an important earlier Macintosh romance.

My information about it comes from overhearing other students talking about it when I was at Yale. I have not had it confirmed. Julian Hartt informed me that there are several versions of how this first marriage originated. I can only claim that my version has rudiments of truth.

Macintosh was on a train trip a number of years after he had come to Yale, when two young ladies entered his coach and sat immediately in front of him. He was so impressed with their conversation that when one of them left the train he made special note of the station. On his return trip, he stopped at that station and inquired about the young lady. She was an Emily Powell. He located her home, and proceeded to make a call. But Emily Powell did not know him and would not receive him. On returning to New Haven, he wrote to her, presenting his credentials. She did not respond. He had Deans Charles Brown and Shailer Mathews of Yale and Chicago Divinity Schools, and President Angell of Yale, write to her. Their testimonials did bring a response, and a romance developed and blossomed. They were married on February 13, 1921.

As the eminent wife of Professor Frank Porter wrote in the New Haven Register less than two years later, Emily was "a pianist of rare musical feeling and interpretive power . . . a personality of unusual charm and liveliness, a genuiune lover of people," who entered into the life of the Divinity School faculty wives, the First Baptist Church of New Haven, the community of Hamden--where she contributed to the planning and, of course, the decorating of her new home--and endeared herself deeply to those with whom she had association. But she died in childbirth twenty-one months after her marriage.

"The following week," wrote Bainton, "happened to be his [Mac's] assignment for chapel. He did not flinch but on the first day, read his scripture from the prophet Habakkuk:

> 'Although the fig tree shall not blossom, neither shall fruit be in the vines; the labour of the olive shall fail, and the fields shall yield no meat; the flock shall be cut of from the fold, and there shall be no herd in the stalls: Yet I will rejoice in the Lord, I will joy in the God of my salvation.'[6]

And in Systematic Theology where he had been discussing immortality, he began: 'What I have been saying stands even more surely.'

In 1925 he married Hope Conklin. She was, I have understood, the other young woman who had sat in front of him on that fateful train trip in 1919, and, as Bainton recounts, she was also a lady of outstanding endowments. Born in Dowagiac, Michigan in 1887, she graduated from the University of Michigan in 1910, and then began a distinguished career as educator at the college preparatory level. Starting with high schools in Ann Arbor and Oak Park, she "went on," Bainton relates,[7] to become the assistant to the head of the Scarborough School for boys and girls in the village of that name on the Hudson. After this apprenticeship she entered in 1919 upon her independent role as head mistress of the Cambridge School for girls. Here, with free scope to implement her educational ideas, she recruited the finest teachers, paid them unusually high salaries, and raised the necessary money by increasing the enrollment. None could resist her [queenly] importunity. . . . As a head mistress she was exciting. . . . Her enthusiasm was innovating. With several others she inaugurated The Historical Reference Bulleting with [Medievalist] Henry Copley Green. . . . Hope permitted one of her teachers . . . to devote most of her Thursdays to research in theHarvard Library. Rare hours were spent sifting things grave and gay--Gregorian chants, carols, Troubadour songs in Latin and French with music'."

Marrying Douglas Macintosh in 1925, she continued her teaching in Boston for another four years to spare him the support of her mother, for whom she provided for forty years. "In 1929 to be nearer her husband, she took the post of co-director of Hamden Hall in Hamden, Connecticut, bringing her mother to Hamden with her. Thereafter for several years she served as head of the girls' section of the New Canaan County School." She also, as Julian Hartt relates, enabled her husband to invite small groups of students to his home. "Mrs. Macintosh," says Hartt, "prepared lavish teas and served them in high style. . . . As seminary students we had been entertained, very occasionally, by faculty people, but not in the Macintosh style."

Continuing Bainton's narrative: "When Douglas Macintosh suffered a paralytic stroke in 1942, she nursed him until his death in 1948. Those years were confining for her, and doubly so following upon so active a career, but she did get her husband out riding and to Bixler's Terry lectures, as Hartt and Bixler respectively report, but as Bainton continues, the "war was on and people were everywhere in need. She began sending packages sometimes to people of literary renown with whom she developed lasting friendships and extensive correspondence," etc.

"Two years before the death of Douglas Macintosh, Mrs. Conklin also became an invalid. Hope nursed them both, and her mother for another eleven years." But even now she declined to be isolated. Books opened vistas; she would center her reading on selected fields. . . . [And] there were contacts . . . with people" and services to human needs. "A young mother came to call and confessed to a sense of inferiority at the meetings of the P.T.A., where most of the women were college graduates and she was not. Hope reassured her that a number of the wives of the Yale Faculty had no more formal training than she and were filling their roles well.

"Hope's last act was in keeping with the whole. She bequeathed nearly everything to Yale University for the Douglas Clyde Macintosh Fellowship in Theology and the Philosophy of Religion. . . . During her lifetime she had stinted herself to enlarge the fund."[8] She died in 1959 less than two weeks after her mother.

Her devotionn to Douglas Macintosh had naturally extended to taking over his correspondence and, of course, telling him about it. She had "assured one of the alumni," she explained, "that he was the professor's favorite son. The stricken man then said

Douglas Macintosh as I remember him.
(See last paragraph of this and next page)

clearly, 'No, three thousand.' That was the number of his favorite sons."[9] I was happily one of those.

    I recall his conversations with me, and his rushing off of letters by longhand on my behalf, because secretarial service was not available on weekends. He was a great personal friend as well as a great mentor: a multisided intellectual, a quite different version of Socrates. I still, indeed, recall the prominent intellectual forehead that bespoke a "thinker," and the vivid countenance that reminded me of Edmund Wilson's characterization of Professor Grosbeck's (A. N. Whitehead's) face, that it was as if one were seeing an unmasked face for the first time. The quiet intelligent magnetisms of both Whitehead and Macintosh have striking similarities. This book seeks to attempt to further disclose the mind and character of the man.

I wish to do this in depth, since he was a key figure in the intense philosophical and theological controversies that marked the beginning of this century. As Randolph Miller has pointed out in <u>The American Spirit in Theology</u>, this was a period when the Cambridge William James sparked the crystallizing of America's distinctive mental temperament and type of thought. James' radical empiricism and pragmatism generated much argumentative discussion and intellectual ferment. Not only did as many as thirteen types of pragmatism disclose themselves (at least to Arthur Lovejoy) but a variety of philosophical realisms emerged of which neo-realisms, dualistic realisms, and monistic critical realisms were most prominent. George Santayana gave literary expression to a dualistic kind of realism which maintained that what we perceive of an existing object is its essence rather than its distinctive individuality. Macintosh, by contrast that dated back to 1913, urged that our actual perceptual knowing is a direct awareness of individually existing objects in relation to each other, a perceiving that is assisted by scientific study and critical thinking.

Macintosh and Roy Wood Sellars were, independently, the first two official critical realists, and it was Macintosh who insisted from the first that perceptual knowing was a monistic rather than dualistic relationship. It was Macintosh, also, who extended this conception not merely to moving, living things and persons but also to minds, and even, in special circumstances, to God.

His impact on his students and peers has been suggested in this Preface from the vantage point of five later decades. An interlude of Existentialism, Neo-orthodoxies, and Philosophical Analysis, not to neglect Rock music, had left him in recession. But a fresh swing of the "cultural" pendulum has begun, and Macintosh merits a full resurgence with adequate recognition for his contributions to philosophy and theology, and to high principles.

I shall accordingly undertake to present a religio-philosophical biography of him that begins with his earliest Scottish type realism and Baptist pietism; moves through scepticism and agnosticism to empiricism, and developing scientism, finds a haven in Hegelian Idealism, becomes disenchanted, spends considerable time with Chicago Pragmatisms, elaborates a monistic critical realism, evaluates the merits and liabilities of the numerous mysticisms, the supportable rudiments in Existentialism, the lacks in such conclusions as those of Eustace Haydon, the contributions of Process philosophers, the extensibility to human values and spiritual life of a monistic realism that takes empirical science seriously, and the place in discriminating faith for permissible over-beliefs. Such a perspective is certainly not expected to be without its questionable points. We shall try to do justice to those while also attempting to give Macintosh credit for epochal contributions.

CHAPTER I

BIOGRAPHICALLY, DOUGLAS CLYDE MACINTOSH

The story of Douglas Clyde Macintosh as a person has been suggested in the Prefaces. Born February 8, 1877, at Brendalbane, Ontario, Canada (which was named for Brendalbane, Scotland, from which his father Peter Macintosh's maternal grandfather had come with a group of neighbors), he was descended from a line of three Baptist deacons. His mother, Elizabeth Everett, in turn, descended from Rev. John Cotton, who came from Boston, England, to Boston, New England in 1633. His father, with the historical New England names of Cotton Mather Everett, settled in Canada, where he practiced medicine as well as farming and skillfully engaged in controversy as a Wesleyan Methodist. Douglas found in his mother one of the two best examples of what he later termed the "right religious adjustment."[1]

He came naturally therefore by a strong religious bent. But his first experience at nine years of age in professing Christianity did not yield a continuing sense of commitment. Indeed, he later thought he had been trapped by evangelical pressures. In his fourteenth year, however, when meetings were held once a week for those who wished to consult the minister about the Christian life, a query from his mother whether he was going to attend led him to the conviction that he needed to gain an authentic Christian experience. He attended the meeting that night with the result that he made a considered, personal Christian commitment. This was soon followed by a decision for the ministry. The degree of these commitments was shown in a letter of twelve closely written foolscap pages he wrote to his older brother, who had given up his chances of higher education for the sake of the others in the family but had then, through his own reading and thought, become skeptical of Christianity. Douglas undertook to convince his brother by "good and sufficient reasons" that the Bible is the inspired word of God. The brother praised the letter yet said that it contained "not one real proof".[2]

The experience of his brother's skepticism together with a number of other critical discoveries led him to the issue of the philosophical bases of religion. In high school he had dipped into <u>Whately's Logic</u>, and he later read J.F. Ferrer in old copies of <u>Blackwood's Magazine</u>. Then, while teaching two years in a one-room school, he read Drummond's <u>Natural Law in the Spiritual World</u> and also listened to a philosophical lecture by a Methodist minister. The lecture began with the sentence: "If there is anything more foolish than for a person to think that because he knows a thing or two he knows everything, it is for him to think that because he does not know everything, he might as well give up what little he does know."[3]

When, therefore, Douglas entered McMaster University in 1899, he resolved to specialize in both natural science and philosophy to fit himself to deal better with the intellectual problems of religion. At the Christmas recess of that first year, he took home, to his mother's chagrin, Darwin's <u>Origin of Species</u>. When he assured her that all he was seeking was the truth and that he did not want to feel that there was anything he was afraid to read, she withdrew all objection on the understanding that he "was to read the book in spirit of truthseeking and prayer."

Meantime, he maintained a correspondence with his close friend and former roommate John Bates. The latter was studying under the Idealistic Philosopher, John Watson, of Queens University, Kingston, Ontario. Enamored with the intellectual and religious riches of the philosophies of Immanuel Kant, G.W.F. Hegel, and Edward Caird as presented by Watson, Bates wrote about them with enthusiasm. His own philosophy, he stated, was a "speculative idealism which was neither a subjective idealism nor an objective idealism but both as well as neither, and something more than either."

Douglas soon also saw the gleamings of rational idealism. Studying Thomas Hill Green's Neo-Kantianism in his junior year, he found that it appealed to his intellectually religious consciousness. Then on reading Benedict Spinoza's "remarkable" Ethics he leaned toward a post-Kantian Spinozism, and was almost an Hegelian before reading Hegel. But in his senior year, while working on Kant's Critique of Pure Reason and Green's Prologomena to Ethics, he began to have misgivings about Hegelian idealism. It dawned gradually on him that a timeless, all-inclusive Absolute (mind) could not be a satisfactory substitute for the living God of religious faith. Nor was he content with the Hegelian explanations of evil as justified from the perspective of the rational whole. Yet Hegelian idealism continued to be his basic philosophic perspective and his key to religion.

It is not surprising, then, that he should begin to be disturbed by the narrowness and dogmatism of some of his teachers. In preparing for his examination in a course on Christian Evidences, he made a three column list of: 1) the professor's teachings; 2) his own objections; and 3) constructive suggestions that he would offer. In the actual examination he criticized the professor's views of three of the questions, then he was pleased to find that although the Professor regretted Douglas' rational idealism, he did not allow his student's disagreement to affect his grading of the examination.

Other professors, however, were more sympathetic and helpful. Professor George Cross, in history, brother of the minister under whom he had made his religious commitment, advised him to read modern theology, as well as philosophy, and notably that of Herrmann. Before he could do this, however, he was asked by his philosophy professor, Ten Broeke, to teach his sophomore and junior courses, while the latter went on leave. With what he envisaged as an emancipating philosophy of his own, he gladly undertook this task, and was allowed all the freedom that he wished. This work seemed sufficiently effective and so satisfying that before the year ended he became convinced that his best work for informed Christianity could be done as a teacher. He must, therefore, go on to graduate study in philosophy.

Harvard was his choice for advanced study. There he could work under William James, Josiah Royce, and their associates. Before going there, however, he wanted to see what there was in the modern theology that Professor Cross had advised him to read.

To do this he decided to spend a term or two at the University of Chicago with G.B. Foster, Shailer Mathews, W.R. Harper, G.B. Smith and others. And he believed John Dewey to be still there in philosophy.

He was disappointed on arriving, however, to find that Dewey had emigrated to Columbia University. He had left a strong pragmatist school behind, nonetheless, in the philosophical persons of J.H. Tufts, A.H. Mead, J.R. Angell (later to be President of Yale), A.W. Moore, and E.S. Ames. That they really constituted a school was witnessed to by William James, who began a visiting lecture in Chicago with the statements: "You have a strong school of thought here." All were Pragmatists. "At Harvard we have thought but no school." The Harvard department was deliberately and stimulating diversified. "At Yale," he said, "they have neither thought nor school."[4]

Finding that he was getting what he wanted in theology with Foster and G.B. Smith, in Bible with President Harper and Professors Burton, Mathews, and J.M.P. Smith, and in philosophy with A.W. Moore, Mead, and Angell, Douglas decided to remain at Chicago. His principle work in philosophy his first year was a course with Moore in cticicism of Absolute Idealism. He took courses in logic his second year with Moore and Mead. And in his third year he had functional psychology with James Rowland Angell.

Meantime he found a point of contact between pragmatism and theology. His work in theology with Foster led to the Ritschlian view that religious judgments are value judgments (in distinction from judgments of fact). This position led Douglas to analyze religious statements to determine the truth of (A.) Ritschl's contentions. Douglas found some religious statements to be grammatically value propositions (as in "Holy is the Lord"). Some are psychological value judgments (as in "My soul panteth after righteousness"). Others are value judgments in the sense that they are necessary from the point of view of the highest values (Man needs God for the attainment of his finest potential").[5] The diversity of valuations in religious statements gave plausibility to the Ritschlian position which, in turn, fitted in with the functionalist interpretations of instrumentalist pragmatism.

The most immediate effect of the combined Ritschlian and pragmatic views was to raise further doubts of the adequacy of Hegelian philosophy for religion, life, and philosophical thought.

Yet his conversion to Ritschlianism and Pragmatism remained incomplete. Statements, propositions, hypotheses, judgments were commonly, in a broad sense, judgments of existence, as well as of value. While the distinction between existential and value judgments was important, it was relative rather than absolute. A beautiful painting need have no near counterpart in the realm of real things. Yet, it is the painted picture which is beautiful and so depicts imagined beauty.

Douglas was more than interested to find a confirmation of his thinking in the theologies of Ernst Troeltsch and George Wobbermin. Both had taken the position, on a more-or-less Ritschlian background, that theology must be taken as metaphysics (i.e., as characterizing objective reality) and treated metaphysically. He decided, in consequence, to write his doctoral dissertation on the relations of metaphysics and theology, though reducing it later to <u>The Reaction Against Metaphysics in Theology</u>. His conviction was, he wrote, that "even from an instrumentalist or functional view a metaphysical interpretation and development seemed clearly desirable and even necessary."

He taught at Brandon College in Manitoba, 1907-09, while working on his thesis, and helped to organize their department of theology. In conjunction with this work at Brandon he read a paper on the New Theology of R.J. Campbell before the Baptist Convention of Western Canada. The paper was a criticism of rational idealism in theology (which had been essentially his own philosophy of religion when he left McMaster). "It is a fact that surprised many," he wrote, "that the theologicaly more conservative McMaster left me radical . . . whereas the notoriously radical University of Chicago left me comparatively conservative in relation to the Christian tradition. . . . The explanation is not to be found entirely in the contrariness of my spirit, I think, but rather in the fact that having found at Chicago an exhilarating freedom of thought and discussion, I soon discovered that what I was fundamentally interested in was conserving the vital values of the Christian religion . . . ." The Baptists of Western Canada, in any case, were satisfied that he had "the root of the matter . . . in him."[6]

His <u>Reaction Against Metaphysics in Theology</u> was published in Chicago in 1911. Meantime with a Ph.D. degree from the

University of Chicago (1909) and three years of college teaching (one of them, we noted, before he left McMaster), he was invited to Yale University as Assistant Professor of Systematic Theology.

Now began his quest for U.S. residential status and citizenship which I have related in our first Preface, and his impact on American students and colleagues indicated in Preface #2. We can limit ourselves chiefly, therefore, to his professional work and relations. In as much, also, as Macintosh told the story of the rationale of his theological espousals in <u>Contemporary American Theology</u> in 1932, we can focus particularly on the philosophical motifs that were the counterparts of his theological emphasis. He was, in fact, a philosopher of notable acumen and originality, as we shall elaborate in succeeding chapters. That philosophy was auxiliary and, indeed, fundamental to religion did not preclude its independent stature and import. Macintosh's epochal tome on <u>The Problem of Knowledge</u> (1915) is but one evidence of this. His other philosophical publications include: <u>Idealism as a Practical Creed</u> (1909); <u>The Pragmatic Element in the Teaching of Paul</u> (1910); "Personal Idealism, Pragmatism, and the New Realism" (1910); "Pragmatism and Mysticism" (1911); "Representational Pragmatism" (1912); "Is Realistic Epistemological Monism Inadmissible?" (1913); "Knowledge in General" (a chapter in <u>The Reasonableness of Christianity</u>, (1925); "The next step in the Epistemological Dialectic" (1929); <u>The Problem of Religious Knowledge</u> (1940); together with numerous reviews. His unpublished "Plainman's Soliloquy" has been preserved in microfilm.[7] Subtitled a Philosophical Autobiography it paralleled what he states in his <u>Pilgrimage of Faith in the World of Modern Thought</u> was the course of his own ideational development. As one of some sixty professors of Philosophy emerging from his classes,[8] I am belatedly assuming responsibility for attempting to give him more adequate philosophical credits. He, of course, was a more voluminous writer than my philosophical tabulation indicates. His bibliography at the end of his essay lists fourteen books along with hundreds of articles and reviews.

Macintosh taught at Yale from 1909 until his paralytic stroke in 1942, living in Hamden thereafter, as an invalid, until his death on July 6, 1948. With his wife's devoted assistance, he did get out for occasional lectures, such as Bixler's Terry Lectures in the early Forties. Besides teaching at Yale, he had also taught at McMaster University in 1898 and the University of Chicago in 1919. He also lectured at Harvard, the Universities of California and Calcutta, Oberlin College, and the Reformed Seminary in Lancaster, Pennsylvania. He was Taylor lecturer at Yale in 1924 and was awarded the Bross Prize for the manuscript of these lectures.

With Luther Allan Weigle, later Dean of the Divinity School, he worked out in 1922 the Ph.D. program in religion and set up the Graduate Department of Religion, of which he became Chairman. He also became a member of the University's Philosophy Department in which, states Hartt, he took his responsibilities very seriously. In their Festschrift, a number of his quite distinguished former students expressed their "respect for his wisdom . . . admiration for his integrity, and . . . love for him as a friend." "Integrity," said Bainton, "was a well-chosen word." "Yes, and more than that his candor," adds Bainton, "he pointed out to me frankly my deficiencies and that helped."[9] To have contributed to the development of such a naturally and dramatically effective ecclesiastical theologian as Bainton is itself a worthy epitaph.

Macintosh's role in the controversy over whether Jerome Davis should be promoted to the rank of Professor "made a great impression on the Yale community." "I wish," wrote Hartt, whom I have just quoted, (to me), "that there was a responsible and circumstantial way of treating the Jerome Davis case, for there again D.C.M.'s devotion to moral principle was singular. He was not a buddy of Davis's; the issue was academic freedom of expression." The grounds, of the decision of the University not to promote their Associate Professor of Social Ethics were officially, I recall, that he had not produced really scholarly writings, but it was generally thought that prominent Yale businessmen had brought influence to bear against Davis because of his public criticism of humanly hurtful business practices. Continuing Hartt's statement: "The people from whom I heard most, in later years, about D.C.M.'s role were Weigle and Hugh Hartshorne, both dead. I do not recall ever hearing Macintosh discuss it (in spite of my close relation to him in his last years). As you know he was not inclined to make himself out to be a hero." Bainton, who was on the other side of the Jerome Davis controversy from Macintosh, has since written me: "When feeling was at its height Mac invited Jerome and Mildred and

and me to have supper at his table. He was determined that personal relations should not be severed. And they were not." Jerome died in October 1979. "As President of Promoting Peace, the society he founded, I shall pay him tribute tonight (October 23)," continues Bainton.

"I too," Hartt concluded, "heard him say . . . that he had hundreds (actually thousands) of students but not one disciple. Well, in my experience of him, he did not teach with a view of producing disciples. In this, as in so many other ways, he was indeed a real philosopher"[10]--opening and deepening philosophical worlds for many. He was this writer's first major philosophical mentor.

CHAPTER II

THE PILGRIM'S PROCESS

I have reserved my own tribute until the beginning of the specifically philosophical section of this essay. I had been given advanced standing at Yale Divinity School because of extra courses I had had in religion--most notably under Simeon Spidle-- at Acadia University (in Nova Scotia's Land of Evangeline). I was able, therefore, to enter Macintosh's course in Systematic Theology in my first year at Yale in 1925-26. It was a surprising and gratifying course, plunging us almost immediately into philosophy. The reasons were evident. Traditionalism is too uncertain a foundation for an adequate religion. The problem is not merely that of which tradition is to be accepted (Matthew, Mark and Luke or John, or Paul, or James, or the "Revelation of St. John," or one of the Isaiahs, or the Patristics, Scholastics, Huss, Luther, Zwingli, Calvin, Kierkegaard, et.al.); it is the imprecise and divergent character of any tradition that is the basic problem. Some principle must accordingly be found for selecting and interpreting the tradition.

What is the principle? One appeal has frequently been to experience, and this has sanctions in both the Hebrew Scriptures and the New Testament,[1] in Augustine,[2] and many Reformers,[3] not to neglect the pastoral modes of the Psalms or the visions of the prophets. But is experience itself clear? Again we have traditions: the traditions of empiricism, mysticism and practicalisms. These traditions pass through many philosophers: 1) Locke, Berkeley, Hume, James Mill, John Stuart Mill, Bain, Mach,

William James, et.al.[4]; 2) Plotinus, Erigena, St. Theresa, Mrs. Eddy and others[5]; 3) thirteen diverse Pragmatisms and other practicalisms.[6] How does one interpret any of these traditions? Does experience contain within itself the principle of its own interpretation? Alfred North Whitehead said, "No." Alfred Clyde Macintosh likened the search for a principle of interpretation to the Israelites wandering forty years in the wilderness in quest of the promised land. They found themselves wandering and continually confronted by hazards or problems. Like John Bunyan's Pilgrim, they turned this way and that in readiness to step out but "knew not which way to go." They had a leader who repeatedly pointed them to the beacon of the promised land and used the clouds by day and the starry heavens at night to edge them on their way.

Macintosh himself, indeed, seemed a combination of a Moses and a Joshua, though in a different sphere. He had, he related to his Calcutta Lectures,[7] been going through a wilderness himself: the wilderness of modern philosophic thought. Year after year, indeed, he had been attempting to conduct his students in Systematic Theology through the wilderness. I personally remember the impatience of some of them when the lecture of their professor left them overnight in scepticism or mysticism or some other indeterminate point. It is to this pilgrimage that this essay is addressed, by using all sources including class notes.

In his theological autobiography, Mac tells of his romance with rational idealism and his emancipation from it, especially at the University of Chicago where pragmatism had sway. He was still feeling the effects of pragmatism when he went to Yale in 1909. His pragmatic orientation was, in fact, a matter of concern to his new colleagues. Two papers he wrote soon after going there gave them some reason for concern. The first, read before a Baptist Congress in New York City in 1909, addressed the question: "Can Pragmatism Furnish a Philosophical Basis for Theology?" The second, published in The American Journal of Theology, discussed "The Pragmatic Element in the Teaching of Paul." But by 1912 it became evident from an article on "Representational Pragmatism," printed in the British philosophical journal Mind, that the element of pragmatism espoused by Macintosh fitted in with such a more realistic philosophy than that of the well-known pragmatists.[8]

In quest of this realism, moreover, he himself systematically undertook the pilgrim's quest in the wilderness, which he was soon to ask one class of his students, annually, to repeat. His monument to this quest is a veritable tome on The Problem of Knowledge, which we shall have occasion to refer to frequently. But we shall start from my class notes and an unpublished 1938 manuscript, now in microfilm, on "The Plain Man's Soliloquy: a Philosophical Autobiography."[9] This begins with the problems posed by uncritical experiences of a naive realist, the person who holds that things are just as they are perceived: the problems of real colors in distinction from the apparent colors seen in different lights; of real sound rather than the variations in sound under diverse conditions; real odors; real tastes; real temperatures; real objects in contrast to hallucinatory objects; real positions, locations, distances. Where is the self in the mirror? When we perceive a stellar body, how long ago did the light begin to come to us to which we are responding now? And what is the state of that body now? How do we know there is such a body? Even in normal perception may not the things we see be merely appearances rather than real things?

In his 1928 Calcutta lectures on "The Pilgrimage of Faith in the World of Modern Thought," Macintosh discusses the findings of the philosophers of human experience. The lectures, he explains in his introduction, are essentially biographical. "In breaking with external authority," he said, "our purpose was to appeal to experience, to examine the facts for themselves. [Yet] the history of modern intellectual progress shows not only a developing body of empirical science, but a philosophy of empiricism from which it is natural to suppose that we may be able to receive some guidance . . . in our quest for universally valid religious beliefs, freely arrived at and adequately assured. Most encouraging [indeed] is the word of that pioneer empiricist, Francis Bacon: 'True unanimity is that which proceeds from a free judgment arriving at the same conclusion after an investigation of the facts'."[10]

Then follows four large, packed pages with extensive footnotes in fine print on the nature and denouements of empirical philosophy. We shall extract essentials of his account.

"From the point of view of what has borne the name of empiricism historically," he wrote, "the mind has certain contents, or, to adopt a more favoured mode of speaking, consciousness is made up of a succession of more or less complete states. These contents of consciousness [according to John Locke] are of two principal sorts, namely, first impressions (sometimes called perceptions, sometimes sensations, and sometimes used as including ideas), and secondly, ideas, or images. Sensations are the impression received by the mind when particular sense organs are stimulated. Ideas are of two principal sorts: simple ideas of sensation, which are vestiges or faint copies of sensations, either remaining after the external stimulation has ceased, or recovered at a later time by recollection; and complex ideas, which result from the combination of two or more simple ideas of sensation. In some instances as a result of a process of 'mental chemistry,' the complex idea does not exhibit the characteristics of the simple ideas which entered into the combination.[11]

"The mind, according to Locke, is passive in perception. It is 'like a white paper, void of all characters, waiting to be written on.' The mind does combine ideas which are formed from sensations, but the mind 'has no other immediate object save its own ideas.' It is characteristic of the empiricist doctrine, in fact, that the 'immediate object of perception is simply the passing show of sense impressions and ideas,' i.e., states of consciousness. We have the beginnings of this viewpoint, in fact, with Thomas Hobbes for whom the objects of the senses are phantasms in the sentients.'

"Following Locke, Bishop George Berkeley attempting to 'forestall a threatened scepticism as to the possibility of knowing material things, and still more to cut the ground from under materialism, made bold to condemn as self-contradictory the prevelant opinion that, sensible objects, such as houses, mountains and rivers, have a real existence distinct from their being perceived by the understanding. 'For what are the forementioned objects,' he asks, 'but the things we perceive by sense? And what do we perceive besides our own sensations? And is it not plainly repugnant that any of these, or any combination of them, should exist unperceived?' 'The object and the sensation are the same thing' he declares, 'and cannot, therefore, be abstracted from each other.' Everything, all the choir of heaven and furniture of earth, has its entire being in its being perceived or known.

"[David] Hume agrees with Berkeley that all ideas of substances are nothing but collections of simple ideas, with names attached thereto. In his opinion, 'Nothing is ever really present to the mind but perceptions, or impressions and ideas,' so that 'it is impossible for us so much as to conceive or form an idea of anything specifically different from ideas and impressions.' The opinion that bodies continue to exist when unperceived was for Hume a baseless figment of the imagination. Thus did Hume outstrip Berkeley himself in reducing entities to perceptions. A self or person was for him 'nothing but a bundle or collection of different perceptions, which succeed each other with an incredible rapidity and are in a perpetual flux and movement'.

"John Stuart Mill, agreeing with [his father] James Mill that our idea of an object is an idea of a group of possibilities of sensation, goes on to define matter as 'a permanent possibility of sensation' and the self as 'the permanent possibility of feeling.' The basis for belief in the external existence of the world is that 'the world of possible sensations succeeding one another according to laws is as much in other beings as in me,' and this, it would seem, is the only basis for saying that it 'has an existence outside me.' Closely similar to this subjective phenomenalism of Hume and the two mills is the position of the later English Empiricists, and of some others, such as Mach and William James."[12]

On the basis of the historic philosophy of empiricism, therefore, we are "shut up to a choice between subjectivism and agnosticism."[13] Subjectivism yields a kind of idealism, the belief that reality is idea (or feeling) in the psychological sense, and hence mental. Berkeley referred to this reality euphemistically as spirit and endeavored to import the wealth of Christian tradition into this spirit, but since the spirit he started from was simply the subjective self with its ideas and sensations, he was not entitled to recognize anything beyond the self, regardless of how outreaching or social some ideas seemed to be. For basic consistency Berkeley should have been a <u>solipsist</u>, believing that he alone exists--or, even more consistently, as Hume evidences, Berkeley, as an empiricist, should not have recognized his own existence as other than a bundle of impressions. As Hume demonstrates, recognition of a mind or self is a departure from strict sensationist empiricism to a rational proposition which we shall have occasion to treat later, while the social element with a world of spirits beyond the self, is a back door importation into Berkeley's philosophy that goes beyond his Lockean inheritance. It may, indeed, bespeak a truer empiricism than the Locke-Berkeley-Hume variety. Macintosh states in his "Plain Man's Soliloquy," that ideas of other selves are apt to force us to take account of them, but Berkeley has no empirical basis for acknowledging their reality as more than that of ideas, without the rational postulate of self-active perceiving beings like himself. As for his recourse to God to solve the problem of knowledge, it is a similar abandonment of strict empiricism--unless it can be reformulated in wider terms. Implicitly, Macintosh maintained, Berkeley is a solipsist as already indicated.

Solipsism by itself, however, is impractical. The belief that I alone exist is a very lonely state of mind. It is also hazardous. Taking it seriously one could batter one's brains out against such recalcitrant "ideas" as rocks, trees, metals; or could suffocate from "ideas" of smoke, gas and water. (There are, of course, modifications of solipsism. The 19th-century German writer, Max Stirner, claimed that he alone existed yet acknowledged others whom he believed were simply objects or ideas to be struggled against or worked with. His was a quasi-realistic solipsism.) Stirner is this author's illustration rather than Macintosh's but a graphic instance of Mac's reasoning.

Subjectivism, indeed, is never consistent. Hume came close to theoretic consistency; while in practice he was not subjectivistic. A variety of philosophical idealisms have, nonetheless, been based upon subjectivism. We shall delve into idealism more adequately soon. But first the other horn of the dilemma of subjectivism or agnosticism. Strict agnosticism, of course, leaves us paralytically lost in a wilderness of thought, feeling and action. A complete agnosticism would mean that we not only do not know where we are but also do not know what we are doing. Sometimes, indeed, this may seem to be true, but generally we seem to have some definite awarenesses and we also seem to be able to validate certain of these.

There are, however, diverse kinds and shades of agnosticism, many instances of which are not fully acknowledged.[14] Avowed agnostics, moreover are agnostic in special ways. Herbert

Spencer's philosophy of the unknowable is a good example. Spencer "maintains that the conflict between science and religion has been partly due to the dogmatizing of scientists beyond the proper sphere of science. If the scientist is sufficiently critical of his own fundamental concepts, he, more than any other, truly <u>knows</u> that in its ultimate nature nothing can be known.' 'Ultimate scientific ideas are all representative of realities that cannot be comprehended.' Space and time are wholly incomprehensible. . . . The case is similar with force and matter. . . . When we consider the concept of consciousness we are again face to face with an inscrutable enigma. Objective and subjective things are alike inscrutable in their substance and genesis."[15] Only the relative is knowable, and, hence, only relatively.

The basic problem from the standpoint of empiricism is that of how the mind can get outside itself to know things other than its own subjective contents. How can it know anything other than sensations, feelings, images, ideas? William James thought he had found a way out, not in terms of actual knowledge but in those of justified belief. Following the W.K. Clifford's assertation that we believe a thing when we are prepared to act as if it were true," and Alexander Bain's "Belief is a phase of our active nature--otherwise called the Will," William James posited what he called the "Will to believe."[16] This is not a determination to believe, but a right to believe in certain circumstances. He states, in paraphrase, that in vital instances in which we have no clear weight of evidence yet have to decide one way or the other because a failure or refusal to decide is a decision in the negative, we are justified in allowing our "passional nature" to make the decision. By "passional nature," James' presentation shows that he does not mean any and every passion but our finer sentiments or ideal values.

This proposal does seem to yield in general the safer of alternatives. But does it offer more than a sop to our moral hopes? It is certainly liable to the errors of wishful thinking and false rationalization. As Douglas stated, "Unless formulated and employed with great circumspection," James' will to believe "may lend itself to the forces of reaction and superstition."[17] Even a man of the stature of Earl Balfour could contend, indeed, that there are no adequate reasons for our fundamental beliefs, either in religion or science. In both cases we believe what we do because of subjective need. "The moral of all this", according to Macintosh, "seems to be that while we may recognize the possibility and even insist on the occasional right of belief in the absence of knowledge in the strict sense of the word, we cannot be too careful lest we allow the genuine right to believe to degenerate into intellectual irresponsibility. . . ." We need a guiding principle to "transform the only too intelligible will to believe . . . into something which cannot be exercised and defended as an undoubted right."[18] We are left, in fact, with the basics of the problem of knowledge and, hence, of defensible faith.

There is historically, Macintosh pointed out, a more critical agnosticism than the types we have considered, and it has attempted to spy out the promised land of knowledge with the view to obtaining possession of the kingdom of authentic reality. The spies, however, are far from encouraging. There are giants in that land, "things-in-themselves," that we can never apprehend or comprehend by normal conscious processes. All we can know is a world of appearances, however, is not simply empirical. There is an "active rational element in all knowledge of phenomena," along with the empircal ingredients supplied by the sensory agencies, and there is knowledge only when this empirical grist is put in rational form. The mind accordingly is like a mill. There can be "no finished product unless two conditions are fulfilled," the working of the mill and the supplying of the grist. So with knowledge, "there will be no knowledge of anything unless the understanding is active and unless it is supplied with the raw material of sense impressions.[19] The finished product is the world of nature as we know it, but it is a world of appearances we ourselves have fashioned. All objects of knowledge are mental constructs, despite the rationality and presumed objectivity of our scientific methods.

There are, indeed, Mac continues, three types of reality, for Kant, which we cannot know. The first is the world as a completed whole in space and time. No such world is humanly experienceable or knowable. The second is the thinking-knowing self. It is always the subject to which objects are presented, never itself an object. The third is unity of reality (God as supposed absolute.) Such unifier cannot come within the limits of human experience. We cannot have the sensory data to fill it out. Nor can we prove God's existence by rational argument. Immanuel Kant, the captain of this critical philosophical group, examines the major arguments for God's existence and finds all of them inconclusive. Critical agnosticism seems to leave us, where it found us, in the wilderness still.

But lo! Kant has words of reassurance. "I destroyed knowledge," he reports, "in order to make room for faith." What he meant, said Douglas, is that "he had to show that the claim to know . . . either the existence or non-existence of any such metaphysical entity as God, assumes the possibility of knowledge independent reality, whereas on the principles of the critical philosophy no such knowledge is possible. Yet while we cannot know or prove anything in the transcendent realm we may be justified in believing something about it if our belief be rational in form. . . ."[20]

Can we then go beyond mere possibility and claim firm foundations for religious or metaphysical beliefs? Not on theoretical grounds. Yet Kant does offer a basis toward attaining to necessity and universality in some beliefs. Moral reasoning, which he calls "practical reason," affords such a basis. Our religious faith, he contends, may become adequately certified if, and in so far as it is based on the moral ideal as a universal and truly obligatory law. The moral law, he asserts, comes to us as a categorical imperative or unconditional command. The first principle of this moral law is that one should always act as though the maxim of his acting were to be universal law. One must always do what one would be rationally willing for all people to do. This moral maxim means further that one is _free_ so to act--though it does not establish that he is free to disobey the moral law. It also, according to Kant, implies the existence of God and the immortality of the soul. The moral law demands that we be perfect, but we cannot be perfect in any finite time. There must, therefore, be an infinite time in which we can progress toward the moral ideal. And to provide the infinite time for personal moral progress, there must be an adequate provider, who is also an appropriate rewarder of virtue. Hence, God exists. "Not only [in consequence] have we been to Mount Sinai and received the moral law," says Macintosh, but we "have been provided with a tabernacle for the worship of God in the wilderness of agnosticism."[21]

Religiously, however, says Macintosh, Kant's reasoning "does not go deep enough. Our immediate moral need of God is not to give us continued opportunity after death to keep on working toward . . . the moral ideal; still less is it. . . to make the virtuous adequately happy in a future life. Our immediate moral need of God is our need of moral salvation, our need of that reinforcement of the good will which can come through religious experience at its best."[22] The specific personal experience in salvation is lacking in Kant. And, of course, his key proposition is certainly not an empirically demonstrable proposition. "Thus we see that although Kant avoided Locke's view of the complete passivity of the mind in perception, he was forced into an epistemological dualism more absolute and an agnoticism more critical but more pronounced and complete than that of his

English predecessor,"[23] and, therefore, with his certainties of faith precarious and religiously inadequate.

Is there another way out? Or are we totally lost in the wilderness of experience and thought? Kant's successors saw what they took to be a bright beacon in the night sky. Since Kant had no knowledge of "things-in-themselves" beyond world of conscious experience, he really had no basis for assuming their reality. But what if the world of our consciousness is our mental construction, the world of the mind is real in itself and has great potential. We need not assume anything else. They, therefore, formulated a series of versions of philosophical idealism. We have already met up with a subjectivist kind of idealism. Do the trans-Kantian formulations offer more hope? We shall deal with them in a fresh chapter.

CHAPTER III

SOME PILGRIM'S VISIONS

The philosophic idealisms were favorite targets of Macintosh's philosophical scalpel. That he should entitle one chapter of his *Pilgrimage of Faith*, "Rational Idealism: The Promised Land" raised the question of what sort of promised land idealism had to offer. Here, he said, we are no longer dealing with a Kantian Law-giving Moses but with a Hegelian Joshua who calls us to "be strong and very courageous"[1] so that we may follow the gleam of the rational idealist's vision. With the real as the rational and the rational as real, the pilgrims have more than an "open sesame"; they have a wand to divide the waters of a Jordan and topple the walls of a Jericho--if, at the same time, they march firmly together.

Theirs was not a solipsistic idealism. It was an objective idealism that included whatever in subjective experience was rational, together with whatever in common sense realistic experience was rationally confirmable. We thus had an integration or synthesis of subjective idealism and common sense realism, with also the disclosure of a larger mind that includes the realities of all our separate finite minds. This type of idealism carries the label of Absolute Idealism, a term which Macintosh reserved for a synthesis of objective and subjective idealisms--rather than just a type of objective idealism. Before I present his treatment of Absolute Idealism, however, let us follow him in distinguishing two major types of objective idealism.

Objective idealism means that reality is mental (i.e., <u>mind</u> or idea) <u>in an objective sense</u>. The idea of mind being objective in any sense other than that of fair-mindedness in judgments has presented a problem for not just a few people; but the objective idealisms, along with the behaviorisms in psychology, have led to the exploring of such seemingly incongruous possibilities. Macintosh certainly distinguished two clear types of objective idealism. The first of these he called a logical idealism. In this the focus is on idea rather than mind as such. He used to say, indeed, under the influence of the British empiricists and Plato, that philosophical idealism was really idea-ism, that the <u>l</u> had simply been put into it for euphony (and the accompaniment of euphoria). But the strand of idealism stemming from Gottfried Wilhelm von Leibniz does not fit this characterization. For Leibniz, substance is a center of force and awareness that issues in the conscious energy of mind; this is the heart of his philosophy. And this, along with Plato and the Lockean development, is a third form of the idealist story. Reality, in this strand of idealism, is a pluralistic system of mental, yet windowless, entities called monads, which are governed by a pre-established synchronization. This is a highly sophisticated, rationalistic view which Macintosh acknowledged in his earlier writing [2] but did not seem to do justice to it as a type of idealism.

The simpler versions of objective idealism include, first of all, the logical type we have mentioned. A purely mathematical idealism is a theoretical possibility--if ideas are the essence of idealism. Various pythagorean and modern mathematical philosophers illustrate this possibility. In his <u>Problem of Knowledge</u>, Macintosh treats Plato's theory of Ideas (Eides) as a logical idealism. He examines the arguments of Paul Natorp and James Stewart which link Plato's Ideas to the Socratic method of dealing with skepticism of the Sophists. "In true judgment," Macintosh explains, "the predicate . . . has value . . . for further immediate experience of the thing of which it is predicated. Now this <u>functional equivalence</u> of the predicate, or logical idea, with the reality under consideration is very far from being an absolute identity of the two. Yet Plato tended to confuse the one with the other. . . . The 'is' of predication was here turned into the 'is' of absolute identity."[3] This position becomes intelligible when it is linked with the Pythagorean doctrine that things are numbers or forms. As a mathematician Plato was sensitive to the possibilities in the pythagorean view, and the researches of Burnett, Taylor, and others have shown that Plato extended the theory of mathematical forms to other ideal types, such as justice, beauty, friendship, etc., etc. The role of Socrates in this extension does not concern us here. In his <u>Problem of Knowledge</u>, Macintosh does not make the connection with the Pythagoreans, though on the basis of studies of Gomperz, Ritchie, Taylor, Windelband, Zellar as well as Natorp and Stewart, and the Platonic dialogues, he does conclude that the Ideas are discovered not constructed by human minds, and hence are "independent realities."[4] Plato's idealism therefore, he states, becomes a logical realism, though if "idea" in the objective sense is the key to idealism, there would be no difference between idealism and realism at this point. There is the question, moreover, whether Plato's idealism fits as nicely into the "Great Tradition" as modern idealists have urged.[5] Plato has numerous facets despite his efforts at an inclusive system, and his *idealism*, as Macintosh indicates, is but one of these factets or strands, however central.

A strictly logical idealism would be highly abstract and reductionist;[6] whereas a doctrine that ideal types are the realities raises the question about the status of the common things of experience and, of course, whether there are ideal types of hair, mud, dirt, crime, evil, and particular lions, and of how the Ideas can be related to each other and to the things of normal experience.[7]

A second type of objective idealism is pluralistic and personal. There have been quite various constructions of it. We have already noted Leibniz' panpsychic monadism with its infinite number of windowless minds coordinated through a pre-established harmonizing by a central or supreme monad. While the monads cannot see beyond themselves, they nevertheless "mirror" the other monads with which they are harmonized, so that they somehow have images of real things. The artificiality of such a pre-established order is one count against it. And, more philosophically, the determinism of the world order conflicts with any conception of the dignity of rational spirits capable of selective choices.[8]

One of the similar forms of pluralistic idealism presented by Macintosh is that of Hastings Rashdall, who "regards as valid the process by which one arrives at a psychological idealism [like Berkeley's]. Solipsism is avoided by the doctrine of a plurality of selves, in dependence on which things exist. The necessity of supposing, on the basis of geology, for example, that there was no human self on which they might depend, proves that there must have been some other conscious being, presumably God, for whom and in dependence on whom they had and continue to have their existence. Thus . . . the necessity of God or some such idea, " as extricator from "the more obvious difficulties of an unnecessary subjectivism."[9] This circle of thought, states Macintosh, is "part of the process of the disintegration of idealism into its elements,"[10] and of a makeshift like that of a "blind man making out by carrying a paralytic one."

The problems of the relations of minds to each other and of justice to "non-mental" entities have been indicated by the idealisms of Leibniz, Rashdall, and of course, Berkeley. An alternative answer is that of Absolute Idealism, of which Hegel has been accorded the status of the chief spokesman. And he has been a philosophical conjurer. With the idea that the real is the rational and the rational is that which is real, he has not only proceeded to show that reality is mental, as in the syllogism:

> That which is real is rational
> That which is rational is mental
> Ergo, that which is real is mental.

He has also undertaken to show that two contradictory statements can both be true, simultaneously. His system of categories exemplifies this. The categories of Being and Non-Being both obtain in Becoming, and those of Truth and Falsity in inclusive understanding. My subjective mind with its illusory naive realism can be encompassed in an Absolute mind, as can the minds of others like myself with their worlds of things. The process of integration or synthesis of opposites is a modern type of dialectic and evidently a wonderful instrument.[11] But are Hegel's pairs of opposites real contradictories? The cases of subjective mind and objective mind do not seem so, if we mean by objective mind such things as literature, art, law, schools and other humanly established institutions. It is always well, said Macintosh, to look for a middle ground, and such ground may have a status that is not simply mental. The assumption of an all-inclusive mind, indeed, presents basic problems. How can the individualities of human persons be preserved within a harmonizing universal mind? Josiah Royce uses the example of two men in a boat to illustrate the need for an inclusive experience. Each man perceives the other and a portion of the boat, but not himself or all of the boat. There must, therefore, from the view of idealism, be an inclusive experience in which the perceivings of both are united. But are all our experiences included in an Absolute mind? What about our experience of ignorance and error, so real in and after science and philosophy examinations? How can they be included in an all-knowing mind? If not, are those experiences simply illusory? Does God them as we do?

Are our occasional awarenesses of independently selective choice at one with control by the Absolute? Is our occasional sense of significant finite individulality one of our illusions? Are portions of our lives unreal? Or is the vast multiplicity of diverse individualities one that fragments the Absolute and, in C.M. Bakewell's words, leaves Him or It absolutely insane?

As for the problem of evil in Absolute Idealism, how can the events that we experience as gross evils be evil to an inclusive divinely perfect mind? Hegel's assumption is that the Absolute is God. Since all events occur within the one absolute reality, what we regard as evil cannot be really evil. It may, like certain disharmonious notes be necessary to the richness of the total orchestration, or like the tragedies in a drama that enhance some majestic outcome. Certainly the possibility of moral evil would be necessary to the choices of moral responsibility in human beings, but is the tremendous volume of moral evil necessary to human spiritual growth or to the glory of God? A philosophy of religion that espouses such a price does not accord with the gospel of love for distinctive individuals. A philosophy that makes wholesale human suffering and degradation a component of the true good is neither a rational nor a moral philosophy.[12]

But for Macintosh, there is more than one type of Absolute idealism. Superrational and voluntaristic idealisms are additional types. That which seems ultimate from a rational viewpoint may be found otherwise from a superrational perspective. Physical pain, for example, may be very different to the ecstatic martyr (or indeed to stoic or the warrior) from what it is to the person subjectively concerned with himself. What is experienced depends on what it is experienced with. Problems are very different to the maturely trained and dedicated person from what they are to the child or the sick person. Depth as well as breadth of perspective is a factor. But even these, apart from the martyr and some dedicated persons, are rational examples. The superrational "rises" to the ineffably sublime. As Macintosh quoted St. Theresa: "A moment of the mystic vision is worth a thousand years of life."[13] But the object of this mystic vision is characteristically ineffable. Macintosh cited the mysticisms of the Upanishads, Plotinus, Dionysius, Erigena, Albertus Magnus, Meister Eckhart, Saint Theresa, Madame Guyon, Mrs. Eddy, Madame Blavatsky, Laotze, and a variety of others.[14] While the mystic experience is one of an overwhelming divine reality, that reality has to be described with such negatives as "incomprehensible," although Plotinus can also say that it is "one." But for the mystic, is there any other? In the moment of the mystic vision, nothing else exists. So the mystic denies the reality of physical world and of space and time. He also denies the reality of evil. The extreme mystic, said Macintosh, may be right in what he affirms: the reality of a divine One. He is undoubtedly wrong about what he denies, e.g., the reality of physical existence and of space, time and evil. Under self-induced hypnosis he has achieved a non-normal focus of awareness which excludes the many normal, analytic discriminations of experience. How, moreover, distinguish valid from invalid mystic experiences? Mysticism is not discriminating.

Mystical absolute idealism, in consequence, solves no philosophical problems, though it has given some bolstering to Absolute idealists who would not, nonetheless, adopt its less rationalistic forms.[15] A moderate mysticism is a different matter. It provides for notable moments of beautific, non-analytic vision and for deference to the higher and holier values. It can be revitalizing and fit in with an otherwise discriminating realism. Can a realist keep it in sound balance? What would be his criteria? We shall have to wait until Macintosh is coming out of the intellectual wilderness to find his answer to these questions.

Voluntarism is a third type of Absolute Idealism. Its focus is on will, rather than on intellect or feeling. Because will is an actively directional factor in organisms, it seems to point to a self-transcending objectivity. It would seem also, therefore, to allow for expressive individuality. Is this actually the case?

The original author of a clearly voluntaristic idealism is Arthur Schopenhauer. "The world is my idea," he says, in opening his World as Will and Idea. Neither perceiving nor reasoning can get us beyond psychological idealism. Yet there is, in Kantian terms, a thing in itself, and we have clues to it within ourselves: in our impulses and desires. This is the basic will within us, and it has its seemingly objective counterparts in the teeth and stomachs of beasts, the natural phenomena of gravitation, electricity, magnetism and all the processes of nature.

"In its inmost nature, the kernel of every living thing, and also of the Whole, is will."[16] That this view should be called an idealism, Macintosh thinks, is debatable. Both sides of Schopenhauer's thought, when taken together, i.e., his doctrine of the world as will and idea, brings Schopenhauer's philosophy within epistemological dualism and realism, though "his emphasis on the idealistic element . . . is very pronounced."[17] Macintosh finds confusion, equivocation, and dogmatism in his position.[18] It is not, in any case, a clear example of voluntaristic absolute idealism.

Josiah Royce's voluntarism is a clearer instance. Influenced by Schopenhauer and his own critics, he propounded an absolute voluntarism in which "all reality is viewed as constituted, in the last analysis, by purpose." He was led to this conclusion by a dialectical process that in the most important formulation of his argument started from the polarity of internal and external meanings of ideas. The internal meaning he characterized as "purpose in so far as it gets a present conscious embodiment in the contents and . . . form of the complex state called the idea."[19] By the external meaning Royce distinguished the reference of an idea to objects beyond itself. But this becomes for Royce a reference to the total reality I "come to know as the realization of my purpose." Royce submerges the cross purposes that not only divide society but also erupt in utterly devastating conflicts, and break down individuals themselves. The evils that men do, moreover, are justified by examples such as the outcomes of the sale of Joseph into Egypt and of the crucifixion of Christ. Yet there was the unanswered query about how he would justify the hideous atrocities of Buchenwald or even the murders of a Manson, the suicides of a Jonestown, the crimes of an Amin and the utter indifference of hurricanes, tornados, volcanos, floods, famines, pestitential plagues, etc. Even the individuality that the idea of purposes seems to admit is surrendered to an all-dominating purpose. Royce's voluntarism, in short, while recognizing another dimension in human minds is a scant, if any, improvement on Hegelian rationalism.

But the resourcefulness of Royce has other outlets. One of these is postulation of the Absolute as a Community of selves.[20] A community is more than an aggregation of individuals in an area. It involves the recognition of common interests and objectives in the light of a common past and of common aspirations for the future. The discovery of this community involves <u>communication</u> in which assumptions and desires are brought to light. This requires interpretation by persons capable of such leadership. It is the interpreter who welds the individuals into a community. The case of Moses guiding and directing the Israelites in the wilderness is but one example. Every individual is an interpreter in his own way, and he is likewise a community in which he interprets himself to himself. "But," says Macintosh, "the self is not a community; and a community is not in any close sense like a biological organism."[21] And the spirit of interpretation, which is summoned up to give the selfhood to reality as a whole is not at all like either an organic self or a community.

Either, therefore, we have the real multiplicity out of which communities grow and which they are intended to serve, or we have the Absolute with its submergence of individuaity, error, illusion, moral and natural evil. So we are back to a pseudo-absolutism or a disguised pluralism--though, as Macintosh told his class, Royce goes down "with his colors flying," a strange figure in the intellectual wilderness.

Still the efforts to resuscitate idealism persist. Is there no possibility of a pluralistic idealism that is defensible? The Boston University systems of Personalism, elaborated by the B's (Bowne, Brightman, and later by Bertocci) have been advanced as the type of philosophy that not only emphasizes personal individuality but bespeaks its highest values: moral, social, aesthetic and religious. Personalism, to begin with, has one evident limitation. It maintains that nothing other than persons, divine and human, have being as ontological realities. To prove this, it has resorted to such artificial arguments, derived by Bowne from R.H. Lotze, as that "interaction between different individuals is impossible, so that what seems to be interaction must be one being's actions within itself; or that the only thing that remains the same thing in the midst of changes is a person."[22] Hence, interaction between persons is possible because God exists as a divine World Ground. But, asks Macintosh, in chapter ten of his Soliloquy, is the World Ground anything more than a verbal or theoretical trick? Cause and effect may operate in a personal World Ground, but are they different from the cause and effect I find in impersonal interactions? The case for the unreality of physical existence is no better grounded than in the other idealisms. And it is not evident that Personalism copes with the problem of evil in a way that spares God the responsibility for it.

"What is valuable in Personalism is its personal realism," not its idealism. Brightman makes his case for Personalism by appealing to religious values but fails to "bring out clearly just what the logical relation of their metaphysical doctrine is to the religious values." "It is no friendly service to morals and religion, however well meant, when their fundamental convictions are represented as resting on improbable doctrines which can only be supported in turn by inconclusive and even fallacious arguments."[23] Personalism is ambiguous and deluding, and fails to do justice to the tough, solid world in which and with which we must cope.[24]

The ploys of non-theistic pluralistic idealism may be illustrated by that of Yale's C.M. Bakewell. Influenced, first, by the rational pluralistic idealism of George Holmes Howison and, secondly, by Platonic and Neo-Kantian idealisms, Bakewell, says colleague Macintosh, seems classifiable either as a personal idealist or as a representative of the Platonic type of abstract idealism. He repudiates psychological idealism with its "to be is to be perceived," as not a true idealism. The real, for Bakewell, is *idea* in the Greek sense of meaning fulfilled. Reality is universal experience. Experience is made universal, public, objective, by means of the *idea*. But, Macintosh points out, universal experience is not *my* experience, nor the sum of our different experiences. It includes all possible experiences, past, present and future. Hence, we have an oscillation between an idealism which is concrete but subjective and an idealism which is objective but abstract, between my experience which is not objective reality and an objective universal experience part at least of which is not experienced.[25]

"The orthodox modern idealistic way out of this oscillation . . . by introducing an all-experiencing Absolute, Bakewell refuses to take." He finds the concept of an Absolute mind grossly problematic. "He speaks [instead] of the "Impartial spectator' to whom we refer objective experience. . . . But this impartial observer is a fiction . . . my own other. The only real transcendent being is the free inner life of my fellow men; reality is the idea, carried up into the ideal, the joint creation of many minds.[26]

"We have no thought," writes Macintosh, "of questioning the good faith of the philosopher [colleague] whose views we are considering, but it may be remarked that all determined idealists would do wisely to note the tactical advantages of some such occupation of different positions during this time of retreat of the forces of idealism."[27]

Idealism has intriguing but tortuous by-paths that come back on themselves and leave us in the wilderness of uncertainty. "Whither then shall I go?" asks the Pilgrim. "Pragmatism is the practical recourse," says some of his colleagues. It is time, therefore, to get down to pragmatics.

CHAPTER IV

RECOURSE TO PRAGMATICS

Idealism may have disintegrated, as Macintosh found in his Problem of Knowledge.[1] Yet it left its residues. Some of these appeared in the work of the two best known pragmatists: William James and John Dewey. The former's radical empiricism and the latter's instrumentalism are both highly tinctured with idealism. The radical empiricism connects rather closely with the psychological idealism of the British empiricists, while the instrumentalism develops from a background of Hegelian Idealism, and construes experience as all-emcompassing process. That it is also called Experimentalism distinguishes it from the Hegelian brand of rationalism, while also disclosing a shift from metaphysics to methodology.

William James is recognized by Macintosh as the first to formulate a "pragmatism." Harvard-trained Charles Peirce had coined that term, prior to James, for a scientific theory of meaning, and James picked it up from a paper Peirce read to a small group of intellectuals in the Boston-Cambridge area.[2] Stating Peirce's idea in his own terms, James changed it to something Peirce had not intended: a theory of truth, and an imprecise one at that. But James' view that practical value is the criterion of truth Macintosh took to be the essential feature of pragmatism. Hence he treats Peirce as the forerunner rather than the founder of pragmatism.[3] Though both men had been trained in science (Peirce in physics, chemistry, and mathematics, James in anatomy and physiology), James moved from physiology to psychology, and then to a "radical empiricism" in philosophy. It was this radical empiricism that determined James' formulation of pragmatism.

James' empiricism was the view that nothing is to be admitted as fact except what can be experienced at some definite time by some experient, and the only issues that can be intelligibly debated are those statable in terms drawn from experience. Experience itself is separable in to consciousness and content. Things may exist outside consciousness as a kind of "pure experience," but until they enter consciousness as certain types of entity their determinate reality is not meaningful. They come into consciousness as flux of sensory contents. Consciousness itself is simply the stream of experiences "run together by certain transitions or relations, which are themselves immediate experiences. . . . There is a feeling of 'of,' a feeling of 'but,' and a feeling of 'and,' and this feeling is what the relation really is or, at any rate, all we can know about it."[4]

In spite of this subjectivism, James is also the source of American Neo-Realism. How he accomplishes this is not our concern here except to mention that James passes back and forth between psychology and physiology with a surprising abruptness, and from a veritable idealism to a common-sense realism, with equal facility. He had a superlative capacity for arresting and suggestive statement. Precision of explanation, however, was not his forte.

John Dewey's idealistic residues are symptomized in his Carus lectures on "Experience and Nature." Though these lectures show some assimilation to the realistic currents of the early twenties, experience is still the major term--the inclusive term indeed--in Dewey's philsophy. But experience is not primarily the sensory or affective thing it is for James. Dewey is closer to behaviorism. Hence, experience is actional and notably experimental. "Apart from behavior [in fact] consciousness is a mere abstraction."[5] Dewey does have a connection with William James, however. What he gained from James, he stated at a philosophical gathering, was not his "stream of consciousness" but his biological conception of experience as interaction between an organism and its environment. In this interplay, experience passes not merely from a "gross," naively realistic form to various refinements depending on the development of reliable experimental procedures; unconsciousness interaction also yields a kind of gross experience. Experience, therefore, is not necessarily psychological[6] in the common subjective meaning of that term. The breadth of this conception of experience presents a problem for one who does not have a panpsychic gradient like that of Leibniz's monads or Whitehead's actual occasions. It suggests an unwarranted extension of an idealistic framework.

Dewey officially rejects idealism; yet makes a negative, idealistic application of the 'psychologist's fallacy,' assuming that a "thing is not, in its existence independently of cognition, what it is not in and for cognitive consciousness."[7] He also rejects the view that "things and relations have significance apart from the particular conditions under which they come into experience," while the agreement of ideas with facts is an agreement of ideas with contents of immediate experience,[8] rather than with trans-experiential states of affairs. Dewey's all-engulfing conception of experience, indeed, comes close to warranting his characterization as an "absolute idealist who no longer believes in the Absolute."[9]

But pragmatism is more than the idealistic residues in either James' or Dewey's formulations. The essential element in pragmatism, for Macintosh, is the idea that practical value of some type is index of truth. Pragmatists vary greatly about how this is the case. William James gives rather free rein to the possibilities. Truth, he said, is a "class name for all sorts of definite working values in experience." Truth, in fact, is the name for whatever, in the way of <u>belief</u>, proves itself to be good, for definite assignable reasons. "Truth <u>happens</u> to an idea; it <u>becomes</u> true, is made true, by events." The events verify the idea. Truth is simply, in consequence, "a collective name for the verification processes." Here, indeed, he comes close to Dewey. James passes back and forth, as we have seen, between subjective and objective strands. On one hand, he states that the "truth of any statement consists in the consequences,"[10] but then proceeds to speak of the <u>satisfactions</u> we get <u>from believing an idea</u> as constituting its truth and of truths mutability. He even states that truth is a matter of convenience: the expedient in our way of thinking.[11] He reacted vigorously, however, to critics who thought his specifications too loose, and refined his view to meet specific criticisms. His genius lay in his suggestiveness rather than in precision of statement.

Striking statements by James have been much quoted.[12]

Macintosh finds William James to be a hyperpragmatist who identifies truth with its function. "Its verity is an event, a process: the process, namely, of its verifying itself, its verification."[13] Truth and the test of truth are the same thing.

Hyperpragmatism, indeed, carried over to other pragmatists, notably Oxford's F.C.S. Schiller and leading members of the Chicago School. Dewey's instrumentalism, though experimentally oriented, lends itself to this same excess. Instrumentalism is the view that ideas are instruments of action in the adjustments of organisms, i.e., "tools for enabling us to get along with things experienced."[14] This is a biologically based conception, and it is interesting that Dewey, rather than the biologically trained James, is the leading exponent of this view, and that Dewey, like Peirce, undertakes to formulate a scientific pragmatism. Science, for Dewey, however, seems a quite flexible conception. As Macintosh quotes him, science is "just the forging and arranging of instrumentalities for dealing with the individual cases of experience." And this is the essence of experimentalism as such.

Problem-solving *per se* is the core of Dewey's experimental logic. All inquiry proceeds from problems. Natural curiosity arises with questions, and questions constitute problems. Problems focus in an organism's coping with its environment. Hence, questions are concerned with adjustments to or of the environment.

The process of thought in problem-solving was analyzed by Dewey into five components: 1) the awareness of a problem; 2) clarification of the problem with the determination and assemling of the relevant data; 3) formulation of an hypothesis for the solution of the problem; 4) testing of the hypothesis; 5) reformulations and further testings until an hypothesis is verified. Verification and truth are the same. Hence, here again we have hyperpragmatism.

The realistic notion that true ideas agree with real states of affairs is construed by Dewey in a special limiting sense. In a 1907 issue of the Journal of Philosphy, he wrote, "the objective reality which tests the truth of an idea is not one which externally antecedes or temporarily co-exists, but one which succeeds it, being its fulfillment as to intent and method."[15] Macintosh gives this example of such fulfillment in his Pilgrimage of Faith:

> "For example, we have been walking along the road at night, adjusting ourselves almost automatically to the familiar objects of the environment, when suddenly we are confronted with something which causes us to stop and think. We know not for the moment how to act toward it; our experience becomes 'subjective,' a more or less confused medley of vague perceptions and suggested hypotheses as to what the object is, or in other words, what further experiences might be expected from it, under certain conditions. More or less tentatively we act upon one after another of these hypotheses until we find one that guides us so successfully and satisfactorily with reference to the at first unfamiliar object that we need explore it no further, but can act toward it as something which we know. The tentative judgment is verified,

> the experience ceases to be subjective, the
> element in the situation which had become
> doubtful and subjective regains its objecti-
> vity, and life goes on very much as before.
> Thus the distinction between the psychologi-
> cal and the ontological falls within experi-
> ence and is purely functional. Ideas, then,
> are instruments of adjustment to the various
> situations in which the living being finds
> itself; they are not copies of independently
> existing things, but tools for enabling us to
> get along with things experienced. There is
> a place for speculation, but only for the
> purpose of developing the meaning of the
> hypothesis; speculation can never by itself
> bring knowledge of the realities of the
> empirical world. In order to know, we must
> test our hypotheses by acting upon them as
> temporary substitutes for further immediate
> experience of things, and see how this
> experimental action works. There is no
> adequate test of the truth of an idea apart
> from the way it works when we act upon it,"

so as to satisfy the conditions of our problem.[16]

The "satisfaction" of such conditions is basically different from the psychological satisfaction that William James had suggested as one of the occasions of truth. It is the logical satisfaction of fulfilling all the demands of a problematic situation, the resolution of which might bring psychic pain--as in determining the cause or causes of a type of catastrophe. The explanation may be adequate, and, indeed, inescapable, but an occasion of acute distress. The psychological term "satisfaction" is, accordingly, misleading.

There is ambiguity and vagueness, indeed, in Dewey's experimentalist pragmatism. "Are we to understand," Macintosh asks in his <u>Problem of Knowledge</u>, "that the only novelty introduced by essential pragmatism is a biological language into which the methodology of science may be translated? Or is it a way of getting the appearance of scientific justification for practically valuable philosophical doctrines by bringing both the acknowledged science and the valuable philosophy under a common formula? This is a crucial point which current pragmatism has left altogether too obscure, giving occasion for the gibe . . .: 'If it is new, it is nonsense; if it is old, it is obvious.' And the failure here is simply the last remainder of that pseudo-pragmatism which--perhaps not too unwisely--leaves somewhat vague and somewhat undefined the consequences by which the truth is to be tested."[17]

This applies, accordingly, to the very nature of the reality in the midst of which the pragmatist must function. The only transcendent reality we can recognize, in fact, is "that which, not experienced by us now, may be experienced by others now or by ourselves and others at some other time,"[18] thus restricting knowledge claims to those of direct human experience. Pragmatism's metaphysics, in consequence, insofar as it has one, is, as Sidney Hooks shows, a vague ontology of organisms and instruments.

Pragmatism finds its worth, Macintosh points out in his 1938 Soliloquy,[19] when it deals with such problems of practical importance as the validity of values or ideas, and the relative truth of working hypotheses. A place can be found by it for philosophical logic and ethics, along with aesthetics, economics and politics. But what about epistemology as the problem of how, in the very nature of experience, knowledge is possible? Is pragmatism's theory of truth more than a somewhat refined work-a-day idea that proves inadequate to basic issues and precise distinctions? As for a theory of nature and of reality other than experience, we have already indicated its poverty. How then can religious ideas have any objective significance or be other than symbolic? And is there not a place for purely theoretic, intellectual interests, like the enjoyment of mathematical and logical relations for their own sake? Current pragmatism seems, in consequence, of distinctly limited philosophical worth.

But pragmatism has possibilities, and Macintosh undertook in 1912 to formulate a "representational pragmatism" which not only showed "something valid and essential"[20] in current pragmatism, but also how it might be balanced by "an equal recognition of the element of truth in the older intellectualism." He gave a chapter to "Representational Pragmatism" in his Problem of Knowledge (1915), and, as late as 1931, gave another to it in his Pilgrimage of Faith. His introduction to Representative Pragmatism is a bit cumbersome in the Problem of Knowledge, yet we include it here as a matter of interest.

> "The position toward which we have been moving," he wrote, "is that in judgment an idea, an abstraction from reality, is predicated of some reality, generally of a reality immediately experienced in the past or at present, either by one's self or others, or at least experiencable in the future. But in the view of the fact that, at the moment of judging, the subject-matter of judgment is not ordinarily--if, indeed, ever--<u>completely</u> presented; and in view of the further fact that it would seem unnecessary for the person

judging to represent to himself what is at
the moment not fully presented, it begins to
appear that predication is such representation as is required to supplement the presentation of the reality which constitutes the
subject-matter of thought; it is, or aims to
be, representation of the reality under consideration insofar as it needs to be represented, in view of its being already only
partially presented and represented, which
latter it is by virtue of previous judgments,
or of similar mental acts. According to this
view, then, the typical judgment would be
analytic of its subject, rather than syn-
thetic, because its subject is not a mere
idea or thought-construct, but an independent reality with its primary and secondary
qualities and relations."[21]

"It should be noted," he continues, "that this view does not involve the absolute dualism in epistemology" we have found in agnosticisms and will find in certain realisms we are soon to discuss. "In all judging there is a duality of subject and predicate, of reality and idea, of represented and representing; but this necessary duality does not involve an absolute [epistemological] dualism and consequent agnosticism." Representation does not exclude previous and further possible presentation; on the contrary it can make good its claims only if there can be and is direct presentation. One who is an absolute intellectualist in logical theory, and an absolute monist, idealistic or realistic, in epistemology, can find no place for knowledge by representation, and consequently no place for the truth of judgments which obviously undertake such representation. On the other hand the absolute intellectualist who is also an absolute dualist in epistemology, while he would make all consciousness, like judgment, merely representative, can find no representation which amounts to knowledge, because without direct presentation there is no touchstone by which the supposed representation may be measured, and thus, if not rejected as untruth, vindicated as truth, instead of being left as either truth or a mere practical substitute for it, we know not which."[22]

Representational pragmatism thus requires an adequate theory of knowledge by acquaintance, which we shall undertake to explicate in the next chapter. In simple language, statements, propositions, and judgments can be shown to be true or false when we can check them by states of affairs of which we can have direct experience. They may represent those states of affairs with more or less accuracy or may misrepresent them. The question is, what sort of representation (or identity) is required? Here is where the pragmatic component comes in. "If, in judgment, we represent what is not at the moment adequately presented . . . our need being simply our need of the judgment for some practical purpose, may it not be that when the representation satisfies our practical need, the judgment is true?"[23] In other words, that statement is true when it represents the state of things sufficiently for the purposes involved in an honestly intentioned judgment. At the same time, the correspondence and coherence theories of truth would be accorded their places in an adequate conception of truth, and that of the correspondence of statements to actual states of affairs would be basic.

Pragmatism itself, in consequence, would not remain unchanged. "For example: if a nation, A, is at war with two nations, B and C, it may adequately serve the practical purposes in the interest of which the judgment is made if a soldier of A mistakes a soldier of B for a soldier of C. Indeed <u>must it not always be, as the intellectualist claims, the purpose to know</u>, the purpose of the investigator, the truth-seeker, fulfillment of which is to constitute verification, and not necessarily the purpose to make some further use of the truth after it has been obtained?

"But then, would not to concede this to the intellectualist necessarily mean the capitulation of the essential pragmatist? Not <u>necessarily</u>. <u>It remains to ask, What sort of purpose is the purpose to know</u>? And as we have seen, what makes one a pragmatist, <u>essentially</u>, is the insistence that, as in science, so in philosophy and all truth-seeking, the idea in question should be <u>used</u> as a working-hypothesis, and the truth of the resulting judgment tested by the way in which the idea works. An idea is constructed to serve, in the guidance of action, as a substitute for a further immediate perception of the reality which is the subject of the judgment; and if, when the immediate perception does occur, it prompts to the same action as did the original idea, may it not be claimed, with much force, that the idea 'agrees' with, or is practically the same as, the perception?"[24] [Italics added in sentence #3 of this paragraph and in last sentence of the preceding paragraph.]

The outcome of this revision of pragmatism is its adjustment to or assimilation in an adequate realism. The issue of the realisms was a moot one in the nineteens and twenties. We turn, therefore, to it.

CHAPTER V
BEING REALISTIC

Most people, despite claims to the contrary, are realists in at least certain circumstances. They succeed variously in living in a world of sticks and stones, cyclones, landslides, holocausts, earthquakes, and feral creatures. Common-sense realism is thus an achievement of the normal mind. Realism is the view that entities of diverse sorts exist or obtain independently of our knowing them. There are, of course, things that are resultants of human knowing: wheels, autos, electrified instruments, formulated laws, tactical systems, and probably some scientific objects. Constructionism is a philosphy based on such types of knowing. But the materials from which such things are created are not created by knowing them, and nature has a vast array of these and of entities resulting from their natural combinations. Common-sense realism recognizes these, and guides the organism in its relations with them. But common-sense realism is naive and eclectic, failing to distinguish the mind's contribution to perceived objects in sensing and in both habitual and imaginative projection, and in retaining incongruous ideas of things. Philosophical idealists have capitalized on the mind's elaboration of its objects, while pragmatisms have emphasized the idea that things are not to be viewed as entities in themselves but as what they mean for human purposes and actions.

Still, common-sense realism has the basic core of value that has enabled men to survive and have degrees of prosperity. Hence, wrote Macintosh, in an essay prepared for a 1920 cooperative volume on realism, "common perception and common reflection, with their 'common-sense' results, . . . are to be regarded . . . as very probably in their main features, essentially true."[1] They can, indeed, be critical and in their positive meaning as good sense--if sometimes thought of as horse sense--they are often astute in their discriminations. Critical common-sensism, therefore, becomes a critical realism. But a critical realism is not *ipso facto* adequate in its ideas of perception. Macintosh conceived critical realism essentially as common-sense realism modified by science. Yet various modifications were attempted in this century. One group of realists, calling their philosophy the New Realism, had reacted against the idealistic idea that because we never know or are never aware of anything which is not an object of experience when we are conscious of it, therefore nothing can exist which is not an object of awareness. But this, said Ralph Barton Perry of the New Realist group, is an "ego-centric predicament" which has nothing to do, logically or otherwise, with the existence of things if or when they are not perceived. Macintosh illustrated this type of situation with the example of sitting beside someone. Because I can never sit beside anyone without having someone sitting beside me, it does not follow that I cannot sit down without having someone beside me (some people are very successful in sitting in sheer solitariness). Logically, therefore, things may exist independently of any perceiving. But how does one establish that there are such things?

Two New Realists, holding that "some at least of the particulars [specific things] as well as some of the universals that are real are apprehended directly rather than by way of copies or ideas,"[2] proposed a behavioristic explanation. The Harvard pair of Ralph Barton Perry and Edwin B. Holt urged that the consciousness of things was a selective organic response to the environment, and that consciousness, as such, was a cross section of that environment to which the organism responds. Mind, in consequence, is a set of activities that are not merely neurological but more broadly physiological.

That these special activities are not sufficiently distinguished is indicated by Macintosh in a statement that "the unique relation of awareness, which is the true criterion of the psychial, is either ignored by the neo-realists of this school, or else explained in terms of purely physical adjustment."[3] W. P. Montague of the New Realist group agreed with this criticism by pointing out that a physiological motion "must be either up or down, east or west, north or south, or some intermediate spatial direction. "How," he asks, "can such a motion constitute what we experience as the 'consciousness of' an object."[4]

Most telling against the New Realism was its inability to discriminate illusion and error. If perception is a direct physiological response and ideas are not involved in perceptual knowing, how can there be errors in perceiving or knowing? Must not an object have all the qualities it is experienced as having at different times and in different circumstances? I paraphrase Macintosh's statement in his microfilmed 1935 Soliloquy: If all

experienced data objectively exist, physical things would be
aggregates of infinite numbers of sense data, including very
diverse degrees of temperature, coloration, texture, solidity,
motion, etc. This is an absurdity, and since it seemed to
become the official epistemological view of the New Realists,
their realism came to be viewed as a failure.

The New Realists' "Program and First Platform" had been
published in 1910 and their volume on The New Realism in 1912.[5]
In 1913 Macintosh responded with the proposal of a critical
realism,[6] though he was not the first to use that term. Roy Wood
Sellars had used it in his writings in 1908 and 1909[7] and had a
full manuscript under that title by 1913.[8] And it was Sellars
who gave the name to a 1920 cooperative volume on Critical
Realism. Six other realists who had been writing variously on
realism versus both idealism and pragmatism welcomed Sellars'
volume when it was published in 1916, and one of them, Durant
Drake, went to Sellars to ask permission to use his title for a
proposed counter volume to the New Realism. Sellars was, of
course, invited to participate, as, indeed, was Macintosh. But,
as the later wrote in his biography in 1932, part of what he
wrote--his criticism of epistemological dualism--was unacceptable
to some of the group and he was asked to delete it. Since, to
him, his chapter constituted a whole, he withdrew the chater and
published it in 1925 as part of a chapter on "Knowledge in
General" in The Reasonableness of Christianity.

The group who published the 1920 Essays in Critical Realism
came to be considered the official spokesmen for critical

realism. They divided into essence theorists and intentionalists: Santayana, Drake and Strong maintaining that when we directly perceive is an essence of the real entity rather than the thing as such; Lovejoy, Pratt and Rogers holding that there is an intentionaltiy about conscious experience that directs it to types of object. Sellars was neither an essence theorist nor an intentionalist, but soon began to develop a view which was closer to the intentionalist though notably more scientific. Meantime in a 1920 Presidential address to the Western division of the American Philosophical Association, he argued for the adequacy of a type of epistemological dualism. Sellars later repudiated such dualisms,[8] as Macintosh from the first had done. For perceptual knowledge, Macintosh insisted, the perceived object and the real entity must be basically the same. We can, in other words, perceive real things.

The essence theorists, he pointed out, were dualistic, in that the essences of things are types and not the specific entities we actually distinguish. And Lovejoy, among the intentionalists, was also, insistently, dualistic. Intentionalism itself, moreover, had relics of medievalist Aristotelianism about it and was too indefinite a conception--though somewhat supported by William MacDougall's sweepingly purposive psychology.

Macintosh's critical monistic realism was first expounded in the Journal of Philosophy in 1913 and then systematically included in his 1915 tome on The Problem of Knowledge. In his Religious Realism in 1931, he elaborates the theory in some twenty steps. The focal point is that we perceive in a complex of activities that include sensing, recalling, conceiving, (imagining), and reasoning. And what we perceive is not just our sensations or conceptions but what they disclose. From this standpoint, the mind is no blank tablet on which experience writes nor an empty room with tiny openings to let in the light, as Locke envisaged it. Nor is it a mirror which merely reflects external things. It is more like a searchlight that actively illuminates the organism's surroundings. But even this neglects the questing character of this activity. From the very beginning, people needed to scan the landscape for enemies as well as the wherewithal of living. They had, therefore, to discriminate things and situations that would service or disservice their physical and mental existences, and that of their families or groups. Their sensations signalled types of object which they became able to identify through repetition of the kind of stimulus and memory of its previous effects. Conceptions entered into the identification, and reasoning enabled them to infer relationships and the probable results of actions on their part. The feedback from their responses to things in diverse circumstance confirmed or disconfirmed their perceptual judgments. They were thus able to proceed with proper cautions and concerns, and to secure or advance their interests.

Macintosh did not, as Sellars later did, use the term "feedback," but the pragmatic element in his philosophy—formulated as "representational pragmatism"—provided the idea. Action is a means of correcting inadequate or mistaken perceptions, and of confirming correct perceptions, showing the relational import of entities (and complexes of entities) in the world of one's body and thus the basic world of one's mind.

Macintosh termed the process by which we discriminate external things "perception in a complex."[9] He thought of it as a kind of intuition. In ordinary experience, indeed, it appears as a somewhat massive intuitive deliverance, or insight, not only involving diverse mental processes but also complexes of objective elements. "Unlike the perception of simple patches of color, simple sounds, and the like, it is the perception of something that cannot be isolated from all other contents of experience . . . its presence can be recognized only in and by virtue of a complex of presented contents. Fairly unambiguous instances are to be found in physical movement, animal life, consciousness, the self, other selves, psychial activities, and a great many more or less complex processes and relationships, physica and psychical, individual and social. These are not isolable as elements of 'inner' or 'outer' sense, nor are they mere aggregates of such isolable elements; rather are they . . . realities of the presence of which we can become absolutely or practically certain by virtue of a species of empirical intuition, namely, perception in certain complexes of isolable given elements."[10]

Macintosh's argument for epistemological monism, based on the idea of perception in a complex is developed in some twenty steps.[11] Basic to the argument is the recognition that evolutionary development has furnished man with sensory and other mental equipment and dispositions that serve his personal and group existence. Indeed, "the activities involved in a) attention and adjustment of sense organs sufficient to make us receptive to stimulation; b) the production and location of specific sense qualities on occasion of specific stimulations; and c) the overt psychological response to the stimulus under the guiding influence of the content of experience, are more or less coordinated, and while the coordination of b and c is in large part an achievement of the individual, the coordination of a and b (the stimulus and responding with the production of sense qualities) seems to have been in the main an achievement of the race transmitted to the individual."[12] This explains why, in spite of the problems posed by common sense naive realism, it is essentially sound, and why in consequence, Macintosh calls his view critical, common-sense realism.

There might seem to be a problem with the intuitive nature of "perception in complex." Our intuitive deliverances are suggestive of possibilities but are not proof of anything. They are often in fact rather nebulous. But Macintosh, we have shown, has given extensive study to an analysis of these intuitions and of their confirmation in practical experience. R. W. Sellars' later referential realism supports Macintosh here, though Sellars recognized no intuitions other than the immediate experiences of colors, sounds, images and ideas as such. But these are not the typical objects of perception. We perceive trees, mountains, rivers, cats, cows and people, along with innumerable other external objects. We seem, therefore, to see through our sensations and ideas to things beyond them. But this is because our sensations are signs that refer to things beyond themselves. Evolved sensitivity and what Macintosh calls racial experience have combined to make human beings (and other animals) alert to signals of dangerous or helpful factors in his body's environment. We thus perceive things as real as the organism itself, and though we are aided by our sensings, previous experience, and thought, we perceive them quite immediately. It is not sensations and ideas, therefore, of which we are characteristically aware but the things that they pinpoint and illuminate. To say, indeed, that we use sensations and ideas in the process of perceiving is not unlike saying that we see with out eyes--or our spectacles. Yet, it is not eyes or spectacles that we normaly see. The "overt psycho-physical response [of an organism] to the stimulus [object] under the guiding influence of the content of sense experience" is to the entity that provides the stimulation from within a given context.[13]

One of the differences between Macintosh and Sellars which we shall elaborate on in our concluding estimate of the Macintosh philosophy is that the components from science in Sellar's philosophy are both more extensive and intensive than they are in Macintosh's. Here we want simply to show the special role of science in Macintosh's critical realism, which, we have said, is envisaged by him as common sense modified in the light of the methods and findings of science.

The problem of knowledge, which for Macintosh was the basic problem for philosophy and certified religion, concerns the confirmation, correction or disconfirmation of what we think we know. "To know that we know [and the grounds of our knowing] is a safeguard to our knowledge; it keeps it steady, free from unnecessary fluctuation."[14] But how can we know what we know? Logical certainty is one way, but this applies only to conclusions from associated propositions or statements. Empirical science is another way, and it builds up and tests evidences, finds regularities, formulates hypotheses, elaborates implications of hypotheses, and tests these implications. A crucial experiment can disprove an hypothesis simply by disproving one of its implications. A confirmatory experiment simply adds an additional support to the hypothesis.

This analysis seems largely Deweyan but Mac's Chicago experience had enveloped him in John Dewey's experimental type of orientation. So much was this so, in fact, that in 1919 he published a book on <u>Theology as an Empirical Science</u>. The key concepts in that book are those of variation and adjustment. But it is to John Stuart Mill rather than John Dewey that Macintosh refers these concepts. He had become quite critical of Dewey, as we shall evidence in another chapter. Quoting Mill's "Methods" of determining causal relationships, he put special emphasis on the one that asserts that whatever phenomena vary in a certain way while other phenomena vary proportionally with that phenomenon are causally related to them. In <u>Religious Realism</u>, in 1931, he states in a single sentence the set of rules accompanying that of experimental variation. He writes: "An indication of something causaly related to a phenomenon may be found either in some circumstance in which all the instances of the phenomenon agree, or in some circumstance in which alone two circumstances differ, and when part of a phenomenon has been accounted for, an indication of the cause of the remainder may be found in the circumstances which have not served to guide to the already discovered causes."[15] Yet all that is claimed for these indications, however, is that they are of "great service" as pointers. But pointers are guides that can be evidentialy successful.

In human affairs and relationships, the factors of variation and adjustment are of preeminent experimental import. We shall see this especially in the next chapter, in his treatment of religious experiment as adjustment. That as Luther A. Weigle pointed out in a class session, Mac could better have used the term experiential for experimental, does not begin to do justice to his scientific emphases. His belief in the accuracy and substantiality of empirical science leads him, to be sure, to attempt to extend the range of the latter to the human limit, without sacrificing its critical discriminations, though in this he was not entirely successful. For him experimental science was the most firmly established kind of inquiry, and for him experimental science was empirical science.

In The Problem of Knowledge, Macintosh does survey philosophies of science from Frances Bacon to his own contemporary Bertrand Russell. "Philosophical Analysis" had not then begun to have much impact in America. It was 9 years later, in fact, that I encountered it in substantial force in Europe. Macintosh was then coming to the end of an erudite career. His Theory of Knowledge, therefore, remains scientific in the empirical sense,

with experiments and measurements as the basis of its precisions
and certainties. "Real science" was for him realistically
descriptive: a matter, in fact, of growing definitions. It
started from preliminary general ones and filled out the dif-
ferentials in accurate details from a multitude of observations
of experimental findings. Hypotheses, based on observed regularities, were the guides to experiments, and Mill's method a
general format for determination of effective relationships.

One arrives thereby, at generalizations or laws of the
behavior of entities, living and non-living, and in diverse
situations. Theories based on repeatedly consistent results are
the goal of science. From these, both prediction and control are
possible,[16] on the one hand, and philosophical elaboration in
terms of cosmology and ontology with philosophies of values,
including religion, on the other. Critical realism, thus, can
provide the basis for the most adequate understanding for human
living at its wisest and best.

Like Sellars, Macintosh recognized different levels of knowing, including a philosophical level, as well as a perceptual and
a scientific level. Macintosh's basic philosophical position is,
indeed, more encompassing than his critical realism. He sums up
his epistemological findings in these terms:

> "Thus our conclusions in the various
> separate investigations which we have been
> obliged to undertake are seen to converge
> toward what is, in general, one and the same
> philosophical position. In epistemology
> proper we are led to a critical realistic
> monism. Obliged, for the completion of our
> solution of the problem of acquaintance,

make excursions into the morphology of knowledge and genetic logic, we found ourselves with a critical perceptual monism in the former field, and a critical empirical monism in the latter. In logical theory . . . we [have] arrived at a critical pragmatic monism, and finally, in methodology, at a critical empirical monism. Our result is thus <u>critical monism</u>, epistemological, morphological, genetic, logical, and methodological."[17]

He continues:

"This critical monism has much in common with the point of view occupied by Hoeffing, and to which he applies the name, but Hoeffing's interest is almost entirely in maintaining his monism in connection with meta-physical problems, and his 'critical' principle is based upon Kantian presuppositions, and is not without its suggestions of agnosticism. Our own critical monism, on the contrary, which in the present volume has been applied only to problems included within the general field of epistemology, departs fundamentally from the Kantian point of view, and looks directly to the sciences, in which, with their carrying of the unifying process as far, but only as far, as the facts will allow, the pace is set for all philosophical undertakings."[18]

CHAPTER VI

RELIGIOUS REALISM

The claim to an all-around realism is distinctive of Macintosh. His was a realism of physical things, conscious living beings, societies, human values, and the cosmic basis and pre-eminent object of religious faith. Religious realism was his special focus. His concern with philosophy grew out of his concern for the secure foundations of personal religion. We shall, therefore, devote this chapter to his philosophy of religion.

The term "philosophy of religion" has two meanings, he pointed out. It may mean 1) the philosophy about religion on the basis of all of its data, or it may mean 2) the philosophy implicit in religion: Is it necessarily theistic, pluralistic, ethical, etc.? Macintosh undertook to combine both meanings and to do so in the light of a third approach to religious philosophy: the inquiry into the religious values of diverse philosophical systems to determine which provides an adequate basis for religion. This was his motivation in the epistemological and other philosophical investigations we have treated in the preceding chapters.

We are now ready for their application to religion. Macintosh, however, was not just concerned with religion per se, though he studied its diverse phenomena: from awe and reverence in the presence of mysterious power--sometimes even the sense of mere magical potency--to the ethical religions of the Zoroastrians, Hebrews and Christians. Sacrificies, rituals, passions, feuds appear in all of them. Crusades are not just distinctive of the Christians. They were characteristic also of Mohammendans. And the records of the crusaders and others is not a clean slate. It has been easy, indeed, not only for Karl Marx to emphasize the enervations of religion but also for such an erudite thinker as Bertrand Russell to become imbued with its feuds and brutalities. The basic question, in consequence, is what constitutes good or adequate religion. Macintosh was concerned for religion at its very best.

At the University of Chicago, in the early 1900's, he became predominantly interested in the place of values in religion. Studying the German Ritschlian theologians' movement away from metaphysics in theology to its value content, he found religion's value stresses to be a focal factor. Religion is distinguished, first of all, by its emphasis on what is worthy, elicits worship. Humanism in America--and elsewhere--considers this the very essence of religion, and interprets value as purely human values. Macintosh acknowleged value as a fundamental or essential of religion but recognized four other features that meet all the requirements of essences as such. They are each "that in actual religion required by ideal religion that will retain its vitality when separated out of the actual."[1]

Foremost among religion's essences, along with its focal concern about values--and, indeed, inseparable from it--is its adjustment to reality for the promotion of special values. "Rooted [indeed] in an awareness of a mysterious higher reality . . . religion first becomes religion in the full sense . . . when it becomes a way of life, a way of promoting or at least seeking to promote appreciated values by means of adjustment to a specifically religious object, regarded not only as a reality but a power."[2]

The dimensions and outreach of religion are shown in the other three essentials. There is 3) the need for **knowledge** of the divine reality with which people seek an adequate relationship. Hence there must be a sufficient revelation, however it is gained. And despite Whitehead's characterization of religion as "what man does with his solitariness," it has 4) a social outreach, since man not only lives in society but his religion has significant consequences for society. And this, in turn, entails 5) social organization and polity, as the history of religion has amply demonstrated. All five essentials of religion, as we have already stated, meet the requirements of essences as such. Each of them is "that in actual religion that is demanded by ideal religion that will retain its vitality when separated out of the actual."[3] Essential religion is thus multi-dimensional, with height, depth, breadth and perpetuity.

It has taken the unfoldings of history to disclose these dimensions. Macintosh does not spend time on those who think that the "word of God" has the same merit from the beginning to the end of their scriptures. There is extensive development to it, and Macintosh distinguishes five theories of the origin and development of religion which do not do justice to it:

1) nativism, with its explanation of religion in terms of instinct;

2) naturism, which emphasizes the primitive feelings of dependence and awe;

3) collectivism, which focuses on the value-seeking tendency (on behalf of the group);

4) animism, which projects self-hood or living spirit into nature;

5) mysticism, which claims awareness of an ineffable something but is not always religious.[4]

Macintosh's own finding is that religion is a continuously evolving set of historical experiments. Having "a double taproot . . . in our consciousness of reality and our seeking of values"[5] religion involves people's experimental adjustments to reality for the sake of the espoused values. These experimental adjustments may be entirely unscientific and yet become more and more discriminating as the histories of religious groups show. Increasing knowledge has enabled men (and women) to discriminate better the nature of the reality with which they need to be concerned and to make their adjustments more appropriate and adequate. It is the grounds of such religious knowledge with which we are basically concerned in this chapter.

As in general philosophy so too in philosophy of religion, Macintosh's approach is by way of the philosophical isms. Though there can, indeed, be faith in honest doubt, scepticism and agnosticism yield doubt and uncertainty and offer no ultimate resource for man. The Idealisms, subjective, objective, and absolute, each has its special problems that range from egoism which may be more or less enlightened to a pantheism in which the person's individuality and freedoms are submerged in an all inclusive, if supposedly divine, being, and hence illusory.

Pragmatism, in turn, has its subjectivisms and humanisms. We have a superlative example of the problems that it poses in the life of Macintosh's memorable Professor George Burman Foster. Mac devotes twenty-two pages to him in a comprehensive 1940 volume on <u>The Problem of Religious Knowledge</u>. The compass of this book is indicated by the "Analytical Table of Contents" which I include in an Appendix.

While continuing to affirm the validity of faith in God, Foster began as early as 1905 to question the effect on theology and religion of the pragmatic or instrumentalist doctrine. In his lectures that year on Christian Dogmatics, he "interpreted Pragmatism to mean that ideas and truth have a functional significance only and are not to be taken as being valid representations of objective reality in any metaphysical sense."[6] The remedy for doubt and fear of subjective illusion is mainly practical; it is to live deeply and fully on one's religious possessions and in the experiencing of their values."[7] The Ritschlians evidently contributed this recourse.

Under their influence and that of Jamesian Pragmatism, Foster seriously entertained the idea that the substance of Christianity is "nothing more" that "loyalty to the values of life." Yet he found himself confronted with his own conviction that faith in God is imperative and that to substitute the idea of God for God is like substituting the idea of bread for bread.

Macintosh summarized that "to attempt to construct out of

Foster's varied expressions a completely harmonious systematic whole would be a vain undertaking and, indeed, a work of supererogation. That was not his type . . . As a teacher--and he was a very great one--his favorite method was to sting his students into alert and sometimes painful activity by firing question after question at them, often without giving at the time any certain indication of what his own position was."[8] A student's notes, in fact, quote him as saying in 1918, "so far we have just raised questions and stimulated doubts. Now, let us get orderly to work."[9]

That Foster was himself still a questing pilgrim Macintosh evidences by quoting a letter from Harvard Professor W.W. Fenn. Fenn wrote that Foster "often seemed to hold opinions concerning which he had not made up his mind and, therefore, was often misunderstood." "I am not all certain therefore," Fenn wrote, "that he would really take his stand with the humanists. I remember that once in Chicago . . . when the controversy between James and Royce was warm, it seemed to me that Foster was wholly with James until he remarked casually that he thought the future was with Royce. . . . I had been misled by his habit to which I have referred and, remembering this, I dare not say that Foster was so much of a 'Humanist' as he appeared to be. He died with a pilgrim staff in hand and nobody can tell what would have been the final resting place of his thought . . .,"[10] except that he wrote Macintosh eight months before his death that he desired "a clear and steadfast religious faith" with "a real God" who was "too imperious to be given up". Foster, said Macintosh, was "a noble and tragic figure, a rare personality of brilliant intellect, deep spirituality, vivid imagination and warm friendliness, but fatal withal, prometheus-like, to suffer the slings and arrows of outrageous fortune, but unjustly, for his intended service to humanity."[11]

His impact on Macintosh seems evident, though not readily specifiable. Mac's own entertainment of alternatives dates back to his McMaster days, yet it undoubtedly gained an increment from Foster, as did his impressive teaching. That Macintosh worked his way through dilemmas more directly and effectively than Foster is certainly clear, and that he found good elements in opposing positions was typical of his genius. I recall, indeed, his discussing more than once the preferability of conjunctive to disjunctive thinking--(both-ands to either-ors) and yet the need of critical selectivity.

Assuredly he found good features in pragmatism while quite critical of aspects of it. One of its good features was the emphasis on science in the Dewey instrumentalist version. Not that Dewey's specific conception of science was adequate but science provided the best attested bodies of knowledge, and scientific experimentation was a reliable means of both discovery and certification.

Religion, moreover, can use scientific method very much to its own advantage. Sir James Fraser was wrong in regarding religion as a transitional stage between magic and science.[12] He neglected that element in religion which is concerned not with control of external nature but with changes in man himself. He failed, moreover, to show that in seeking inner spiritual aid in religious ways, man must necessarily be unscientific. Indeed, if it be a fact that religion at its best is of real help toward a better way of living, the truth may well be that one cannot be completely scientific if he refuses to make any use whatever of the resources of experimental religion for the solution of his practical life problems. Religion has, indeed, its own experimental way of life, but this is not to be construed in opposition to science as such, as traditionalists feeling have thought, but in conjunction with it. It is man's variously informed trial-and-error quest for the most meaningful adjustment to the ultimate forces that affect his life.

Macintosh's <u>Theology as an Empirical Science</u> is his preliminary elaboration of his findings regarding the role of science in religion. The focal conception of that book was that of experimental religious adjustment. By dispassionate observations of one's own adjustments to divine reality--along with one's observations of the effects of adjustments in other people's lives, one can arrive at laws of dependably right adjustments and dependable divine behavior.

Not only, in fact, are people learning from such experiences "what religion is good for as well as what it is not good for; they have been learning, slowly but surely, to depend upon divine power in the special ways characteristic of religion, not for such 'answers to prayer' as would involve a suspension of the laws of nature, but for such <u>effects</u> of true prayer in the life of the spirit . . . as experience teaches them they may expect on condition of a definite type of religious adjustment."[13] Religion's science and general experimental science may thus be extensions of each other, as suggested in Chapter V.

In his Religious Realism, Macintosh summarizes his findings about the experimental development of religion. We quote at some length:

> "Thus as a result of experiment, observation and reflection, historical religion in its more progressive forms has been tending to seek preparation for crises, deliverance from actual and threatened evil, and positive achievement and success in life, less and less along lines of direct intervention on the part of the mysterious power in the external world, and more and more in the direction of inner readjustment and integration and the development of a good and efficient will. It is true that, becoming more moral in his interest, man has come to be more interested in the possibilities of promoting moral values through religious experience; but, in this realm of the spirit in his religious life, man has been fundamentally influenced by the discovery that it is in the latter rather than in the former sphere that he can reasonably look for dependable results on condition of a specifically religious adjustment."

> "Thus, progressive experimental religion has been becoming at once more rational and more moral, more spiritual and more scientific. This is not to say as yet that the religious man really does get, through religious experience, any scientific knowledge about an independently existing God; for the present I am satisfied to point out that, within the limits of his realistic religious presuppositions, the religious man, in becoming more critically empirical and logical, is becoming less unscientific and more scientific, and that certain results of his religious experience and logical thought naturally seem to him to yield genuinely verified knowledge of a really existent God. . . .

> "The specifically religious adjustment
> [as such] . . . begins in aspiration toward
> an ideal of higher moral and spiritual
> attainment, not only as an ultimate end in
> itself but also as instrumental to the
> redemption and regeneration of society. It
> culminates in self-surrender, appropriating
> faith and a habitual willed responsiveness
> toward an object regarded as at once ideal
> and real, friendly and accessible, efficient
> and for one's religious need sufficient.
> Such a religious adjustment, it is claimed,
> makes dependably toward the desired result."

Macintosh enters a refinement there. "It is important at this point," he writes

> that one possible source of misunderstanding
> be removed. What is claimed for religious
> experience on condition of this 'right reli-
> gious adjustment' is not an exact, quantita-
> tively predictable result. There may, in-
> deed, be almost no noticeable result unless
> the qualitatively right adjustment is main-
> tained with a high degree of intensity (con-
> centration of attention) and persistence.
> Otherwise the desired result may be inhibited
> by any one of a number of adverse factors, or
> by a combination of several or all of them.
> Among such adverse factors are an unfavorable
> social environment, antagonistic instincts or
> 'drives', deeply ingrained contrary habits,
> ideas and prejudices of an opposite tendency,
> repressed complexes giving rise to hindering
> processes, an abnormal supply of hormones
> from the 'glands regulating personality',
> lack of energy through malnutrition, and
> pathological conditions in general, whether
> physical, mental or social. On the other
> hand the normal tendency of the 'right re-
> ligious adjustment' may be rather suddenly
> reinforced by the release from the uncon-
> scious of the energy and emotion associated
> with a long repressed but growing conviction
> as to truth or duty or a new religious life.
> In some instances this reinforcement seems to
> have been sufficient to overpower and sub-
> merge completely the impulses of depraved
> appetite and to nullify in large measure the

> influence of an unfavorable social environment. But whether inhibited or accelerated in the particular instance, <u>there is, it is claimed a dependable tendency toward a universally desirable moral and spiritual result on condition of an earnest and persistant maintenance of the specific religious adjustment to which we have referred.</u>"[14] [Italics added.]

As I indicated in Chapter I, Macintosh found in his mother a distinctive example of the right religious adjustment. In his autobiography, "Toward a New Untraditional Orthodoxy," he also includes Yale's Henry B. Wright. In <u>Religious Realism</u>, he continues that a clear case of religious adjustment occurs in religiously moral conversion. In

> "vital religion of moral redemption there tends to occur a spiritual or ethico-religious crisis, in which, if spiritual disaster is to be avoided, an experience of regeneration or renovation of the moral will seems imperative, and, as a necessary means to this end, a wholehearted decision and act of turning to God in order the more effectively to be turned from recognized evil and toward the true good. Presupposed in this momentous decision and act is the thought of God as great enough and favorable enough to man to be ready to respond effectively to the right religious adjustment along lines of man's imperative need. When, after a life relatively irreligious (or wrongly religious) and characterized by moral failure, man in his spiritual crisis has recourse with God, entering whole-heartedly into the religious adjustment described and persisting therein, he eventualy experiences a moral conversion of will and spirit which he tends very naturally to interpret as being, in its essentials, the work of the God to whom he adjusted himself. At the same time he is led to feel that such an experience is universally valid and imperative."[15]

But what do we really know about God? An experimental science of religion yields only such laws or generalizations as that "on condition of the right religious adjustment, with a view to being turned permanently from sin to God and to the right way of living, a dependable Factor works primarily in the will and ultimately in nature more generally the definite and manifest beginning of a new and better type of life."[16] Hypotheses may, indeed, be formulated on the basis of such laws and the hypotheses may be empirically tested by confirmation or disconfirmation of its implications. Disconfirmation shows the inadequacy of the hypothesis in its present form, while confirmation simply adds an additional support of its plausibility. All that we know of God, therefore, from the standpoint of a science of religion is that there is a dependable "higher power" that supports us on occasion, and affects our world through us.

We can thus know what Professor H.T. DeWolfe of my Acadia College days used to refer to as God's "hinder parts." Citing Exodus 33:22-23 (where Moses asks God to show him his face), he quoted God's response: "I will put thee in the cleft of the rock and will cover thee with my hand while I pass by; and I will take away my hand and thou shalt see by back parts, but my face shall not be seen." All that we can objectively perceive of God is his effects in others and in the world.

A crucial question, therefore, is that of which effects to attribute to God; hence of knowing more of God as a basis for our attributions. The face of God, Dr. DeWolfe said discerningly, is Jesus Christ. We do seem to sense the divine especially in the qualities that humans in their finest hours reveal. Jesus, for many, was the epitome of that which we find to be divine. Yet here again we are faced with the question of how do we know this to be factually certain.

How can our philosophical isms be of any help here? The idealisms, Macintosh found, trade on the ego-centric predicament wherein because there can be no object as such without it being an object for a subject, it is claimed, and therefore, that nothing can exist which is not an object for a subject. Hence the physical universe is correlative of mind, and thus mind-dependent. But as Macintosh illustrated, I can sit down without having anyone beside me, though I cannot sit beside anyone without having someone beside me. There is similarly no logical reason why things cannot exist without being objects for any mind. That we cannot directly know of any such cases, because in knowing them they are objects for a subject, does not alter this possibility, above all since there are many instances in which discovered objects give evidence of a long evidently unobserved history.

That the idealisms have had recourse to an absolute all-inclusive mind is like a fall into an underworld of drugpushers, God then becomes the depository of, and so responsible for, all evil. And human individuality and choice are lost in the absolute. How, indeed, can God, the all-knowing mind, have my experiences of ignorance and error? Yet, these are very real experiences to me not only on college examinations, but in my profoundly real life predicaments. How could such experiences possibly be part of an all-knowing experience? To have such human experiences the pluralistic idealist Charles M. Bakewell said, God would be so disintegrated as to be positively insane.

Macintosh, who had been an Absolute Idealist, on going to the University of Chicago, confronted <u>pragmatism</u> there. The pragmatists were sharply critical of the idealists. But did they offer a (really) better perspective? Essentially pragmatism holds that that idea which works is true. But the pragmatists had trouble in determining what kind of working establishes the truth of a proposition. Practically, they were more realistic than the idealists, but their practicalities were not sufficiently discriminating. The hyperpragmatists went to uncritical excesses in their claims to truth.

Religiously, Eustace Hayden was an <u>enfant terrible</u> of this group. Religion, for him, was the cooperative quest of the good life, and God was but a symbol of our highest values. The truth of our belief in him consists in the working value for us of our belief in him. "The parent God, guardian of life and giver of immortality, is [actually] no more."[17]

John Dewey and Henry N. Wieman held more balanced positions. Macintosh debated with Wieman in 1932 in <u>The Christian Century</u>. We shall first, therefore, state Macintosh's treatment of Wieman's conception of God. God, said Wieman, is "that something, however unknown, which would and which does bring human life to the largest fulfillment when proper adjustment is made to it." We "know with certainty" that such a being is truly existent in the total environment with which we interact" and that "its goodness transcends the goodness of everything else in the universe."[18] The last point seems either a subjective valuation, or a postulate, or, at best, a "probable" inference--rather than a certainty.

But how different now are these basic elements of Wieman's from those of Macintosh's philosophy of religion? Both conceive of God as "that in the universe which yields the highest values when the right adjustment is made to it."[19] But the adjustments that Wieman provides for could be almost entirely psychological and social rather than specifically religious. Hence Macintosh states that when, indeed, God is so defined "that every person who has hitherto denied the existence of God can now affirm it without changing in the slightest degree either his opinions or his life, the way seems open to become or remain what has always been termed an 'atheist' without any longer having to endure such an epithet."[20] Wieman's God, however, is a force or set of forces rather than a symbol. Is Wieman's statement any improvement on Dewey's?

The word "God," states Dewey in his <u>Common Faith</u>, denotes "the unity of all ideal ends arousing us to desire and action." There are "forces in nature and society that generate and support" these ideals, and it is to the "active relation between the ideal and actual" to which Dewey gives the name "God." "The community of causes in which we, together with those not born, are enmeshed is widest and deepest symbol of the totality of being the imagination calls the universe" and "the matrix within which our ideal aspirations are born and bred,"[21] to point direction and shape our purposes. The idea of God is one of ideal possibilities that are unified through imaginative realization and projection. Functionally it is connected with all the natural forces and conditions--including man and his associations--that promote the growth of the ideal. The term "God" is, accordingly, a symbol but, in contrast to Haydon's "God," it is a symbol with a cosmic basis as well as ideal import.

Dewey's statement is more rhetorical than Wieman's and less immediately relevant to our daily living. Despite the influences of Hocking and Whitehead on Wieman, his statement seems to be a rather realistic translation of Dewey's position. The same criticism applies, therefore, to Dewey's conception of God that Macintosh made of Wieman's theology. But in his <u>Problem of Religious Knowledge</u> Macintosh carries his criticism farther. He wrote

>". . . [E]nough has been set down to show that the philosophy (Dewey's), viewed as a 'rationalization' of the rejection of the theistic type of religion and carrying with it a repudiation of the characteristic traditional problems of metaphysics and epistemology, is very far from being a proof or even a reasonable justification of his religious position. Like all other forms of the philosophy of 'pure experience', Dewey's immediate empiricism is a more or less disguised after-effect of an original fallacious analysis of conscious experience. The universal <u>relatedness</u> of the objects to consciousness or the subject was takeen to involve a universal dependence of the object upon the subject--a very natural fallacy where consciousness is imagined to be an area instead of being, as awareness, a unique relation between a subject and its objects.

> The unsatisfactoriness of subjectivism, both practically and theoretically, instead of leading to a retracing of steps and correction of the original fallacious psychologism, has driven many to the so-called radical empiricism in which the dependence of the object on the conscious subject is obscured by the psychological idealism being applied to the subject as well as to the object of consciousness."[22]

The individual per se is lost in the experience; God, in turn, is simply "some content of experience in which religious interest is taken, not anything real beyond the bounds of human experience."[23]

G.B. Foster's wrestling with current pragmatic humanism was a living out of the insufficiency of that ism: We, therefore, need an adequate religious realism, but not the realism of either the new realist or the dualistic critical realists. The neo-realists, such as Samuel Alexander, wrote Macintosh, are on

> "scientific grounds when they describe the progressive emergence, in the course of evolution, of consciousness, intelligence, and personality; and one may go even further and claim essentially scientific knowledge of God as the principle of emergent evolution, if we mean by that term simply whatever creative principle is necessary to explain this progressive emergence of new and higher forms of existence. . . . But when Alexander speaks of this principle . . . not only as a _nisus_ toward the forms [of existence], that have appeared but as a '_nisus_ toward deity' he becomes not only unscientific but fantastical. . . . What might have been asserted with scientific justification was the existence of a _nisus_ toward a divine humanity, i.e., toward a humanity with divine qualities in the character of the individual and society ('the kingdom of God').[24]

Macintosh conceived the value-producing process as such a <u>nisus</u>.

As for the dualistic critical realisms, they are scarcely in a better way than the theologians of crisis theology: Barth, Brunner and Gogarten. To these theologians, God, although persona, remains forever transcendent, and except for an alleged supernatural revelation in 'the Word,' unknowable. "But why should we be asked to take this 'either-or' [of transcendance or immanence] instead of 'both-and.' Is it too much to suppose that we can both scientifically know the immanent God, Producer of highest values, and rationally believe in the transcendent, essential personal God, Conserver of highest values, and that these two . . . are ultimately not two different things but somehow organically and dynamically one."[25]

There is, however, a realistic alternative. Monistic critical realism, Macintosh finds, is such an alternative. While experimental religion can only objectively give us laws of dependable behavior, and "perception in a complex" is less analyzable for religious experience than for mundane relations, one may have an immediate perception of a divine reality plus cumulative evidences that support, enlarge upon, and fill out that experience.

The great mystics have claimed such an experience. In his <u>Problem of Religious Knowledge</u>, Macintosh surveys 15 of these from Plotinus, Eckhart, Tayler to Madame Guyon and Rada Krishnan (see "Analytical Table of Contents" in the Appendix). He discusses the impressiveness and certitude of the mystic's experience, the rationalizations of the mystics, the questions of their hallucinations and pathology, the role of the subconscious in mysticism, yet its practical value, and probable truths.

He wrote,

> "It is not to be denied that in some instances the constitution of the mystic on the condition he (or, perhaps more frequently, she) is in at the time of the experience . . . has been pathological. St. Teresa, whose own physical health was not always perfect, has this to say of some others who came under her observation: 'Some persons, being weakened with severe penances, prayer, or watchings, or having naturally a weak constitution, swoon away on receiving these consolations, and their nature fails them, and when they perceive some internal delight with a certain external decay and anguishing, or when a spiritual sleep, as it is called happens, allow themselves to be absorbed, and the more they yield the more they are absorbed, and the more they yield and the more they are absorbed . . . and in their idea it seems to be a rapture, but I call it a stupidity, for it is nothing else but losing our time and destroying our health'."[26]

Yet St. Teresa is able to say of her own illuminations that a moment of the mystic vision is "worth a thousand years of life."[27]

There can, in consequence, be highly significant practical value to mysticism regardless of the truth of its claims. Macintosh finds both good and bad practical values. It may tend toward complete preoccupation with the contemplative moment with no disposition to do anything about the neds of oneself or others, and in its absorption with the object of mystic vision, it may, indeed, deny the reality, accessibility and sufficiency of God as to make religion strongly dynamic in everyday life."[28]

Thus on the one hand, there can be acute self-hypnosis, while, on the other, one can have an uplifting, illumination and energizing of life. A discriminating mysticism could be discerningly and even critically realistic. Its role in religion at its best and place in life at its most adequate would be impressive evidence of its plausibility.

Mysticism, indeed, has something in common with Existentialism: the idea of confrontation. The latter came to Yale in the 1930's in the person of Richard Niebuhr. Both he and his older brother, Reinhold, had been students of Macintosh and both had developed theologies that were sharply at odds with that of their mentor. Richard had a substantial impact at Yale, reportedly taking the limelight away from Macintosh. He was, nonetheless, one of the contributors to the Festschrift honoring Macintosh in 1937. The latter's response to Richard's essay is illuminating.

Richard's key charges against Macintosh's theology were that:

1) Religion cannot be intelligibly, much less scientifically, empirical. It is concerned with relations to the totally transcendent, and human conceptions (based on experience) are not even approximations;

2) You cannot get to God by way of human values. God is the source and determiner of value, and, hence, beyond value;

3) Macintosh is an eclectic in combining the empirical and value approaches to theology.

Niebuhr, says Macintosh, is a profound and original scholar who has shown great promise but has gone askew under the influence of Kierkegaard, Barth, Brunner, Unamuno and "others more or less like them." He has nonetheless criticized positions more extreme than his own, and Macintosh is hopeful that his present stance is temporary. He has, moreover, in support of irrationalism, had recourse to rationalism, i.e., employing a one-sidedly rationalist critique of rationalism. Such a critique assumes its own merit and so justifies some mode of rationality. Macintosh followed up with a review of the merits (and limits) of different modes of rationality and of their possibilities for religious thought. There is a level, indeed, at which one can be scientific about religion: the level of dependable responses and "laws". But one needs to go well beyond this, to the conception of a personal God. Our recognition of and concern for spiritual values, including those of personality at its best, points a way. The God we need is a personification of all ideal values, as well as a source of dependable responses. And he is conserver of those values. Moral optimism is an essential attitude for best living, and it entails a faith in such a being. Macintosh developed this concept in his <u>Reasonableness of Christianity</u> in 1925.

As for the charge of electicism, Macintosh makes a more precise statement of religion's bases.

> "I have sometimes used the term 'fundamental religion' for devotion to spiritual values (values which are absolute, eternally valid, 'divine' in the sense of being worthy always of absolute devotion), and the term 'experimental

religion' for dependence and practical adjustment (prayer, trust, etc.) toward supreme being, but I have always insisted that the latter belongs to the [very 'quint]essence' of religion. Perhaps it would have been less misleading if I had used the terms spirituality and religion to indicate this distinction, although I regard my former usage as very defensible. With this change of terms I would say that, while much spirituality has come out of religion, especially out of religion which is already to some extent spiritual, it is also true that there are other roots of spirituality besides characteristic experimental religion. And if we had to choose between the two (which fortunately we don't), it would be better to choose spirituality without religion than religion without spirituality. Spirituality without religion is deficient in dynamics; religion without spirituality is defective in direction.

"If all this be 'electicism,' let my critics make the most of it. I do not think it involves electicism in any objectionable sense. Religion is means as well as end, and as in the case of art and friendship the appreciative contemplation of objects or persons as ends generally grow out of experience of their value as means, so it is, generally speaking, in religion. Disinterested worship of God as end commonly grows out of gratitude for what is regarded as his grace and goodness to us. And, may I ask my critic, Is the objectivity of scientific investigation necessarily vitiated when the investigator is interested in the possible value of his results, as in engineering and medical science and educational psychology? As a matter of fact, the practical importance of his problem may make the investigator all the more careful lest he be deceived. It seems to me that the objection to regarding religion as instrumental to other spiritual values (as well as being itself of intrinsic value) would be justified only if it were, in fact, true that religion has no value for morality or any other spiritual value. That this is the case I do not believe that Mr. Niebuhr himself would maintain. I am not at all intimidated or driven out of countenance, therefore, by the insinuation that an empirical theologian who is interested in values is thereby incapacitated from giving a straightforward, scientifically accurate report of the facts. . . . The temptation to let 'wishful thinking' tamper with the record must always be guarded against, but this is no temptation but such as is common to observers, and it is gratuitous to assume that it is only in all other cases except that of the theologian that, with the temptation, there will be provided a way of escape, so that he may be able successfully to endure it. . . ."[29]

But, asserts Macintosh, "let me make it doubly clear how willing and even anxious I am that irrationalism be given its due. There is always, as an empiricist I maintain, more in the concrete subject-matter of our ordinary judgments than we can get completely into any predicate, even a true predicate, or into any number of abstract predicates. But our judgments may be true, even if they never amount to the whole truth. And when the reactionary 'dialectical' theologians discount all our value-judgments as being inevitably deflected from God's truth by the corrupting influence of 'original sin,' only this much should be conceded to them, namely, that evil desire does often tend to make our reasoning a misleading 'rationalization' of what we want to do, so as to make it look like we <u>ought</u> to do, and that a thorough moral conversion of the will may be needed to clarify the judgment as to good and evil, right and wrong. But in the realm of logical values especially, and the same thing might be said of much that belongs to other realms, the influence of the imperfect moral will to the valuation process is negligible. Two and two makes four, whether your will is good or bad. The judgment that no human value judgment can be quite true is self-refuting, for this judgment itself is a value judgment. . . .

"The existential theologian is on defensible ground [however] when he insists that, instead of violently forcing the facts into the mold of our prior religious conceptions, we should let ourselves be taught by reality what God is. Just so; <u>but unless one has</u>

> learned, through acquaintance with a
> dependable, ever-assessible, divinely
> functioning power, to distinguish between the
> divine factor and factors which are very far
> from being divine, the result of being taught
> by reality (nature and history) what God
> is may prove very confusing and misleading."[30]
> (Italics added.)

How we may be able to envisage God is preliminarily, though only very preliminary, suggested by the evidence of mystic experiences. These could be, when properly analyzed and stripped of excesses, special cases of what Macintosh called "perception-in-a-complex.": a seeing through the complexities of nature and life to the Power and Providence that expresses itself in the universe and its events. And yet this perception is very different from physical perceptions which have a direct reference to things that can be repeatedly checked. Even the more fused esthetic perceptions can point to patterns, lines, and hues to support their claims. While all that the mystic seems to be able to say is that God is inefable and overawing. The idea of seeing God other than through things and developments seems, therefore, a blind faith, but the feeling of the presence of God even among the desolations of the moon, along with both the personal and historic experiences of companionship with God that have been insistently attested, point to what comes close to perception. Hence a moderate, discriminating mysticism, supplemented by science and practical common sense, provides intelligibly for the irrational surds of experience and offers the possibility of rising to an informed vision of God and of his relationships to persons and things. Macintosh's conception of perception-in-a-complex permits this development, though he does not use this term in his Problem of Religious Knowledge. He writes, instead, of intuitions that may be increasingly refined and supported.[31]

Macintosh's theology, built on a sensitive, yet realistic and discriminating elaboration of "progressive experimental religion," bespeaks the achievement of a real vision with greater understanding of God's greatness, goodness, and love. Earlier in this Chapter, I outlined the procedures by which Macintosh urged that we could gain knowledge of God. More roundly philosophical than his critics, he was also as profoundly religious as any of them, along with his religious openness. This is attested to by his biblical approach to his personal and social religion, his devout religious practice, insistent belief in personal immortality,[32] repeated assertions that what is vital in religion is its evangelical experience and disposition, and his basic orthodoxy. His was a remarkable intellectualist piety that did not permit him to be satisfied with the partialities and distortions of God and religion that passed for religious currency.[33] His own theology was built up with intensive care.

In summary, I shall quote from his review of Charles Hartshorne's Man's Vision of God and the Logic of Theism. "As I conceive of a valid theology," he wrote, "it is divided into three principal parts, or stages: empirical theology, setting forth as knowledge what can be discovered about a divine reality through religious experience; normative theology, a critical

<u>Dogmatik</u> of Christian or some other historical or contemporary faith; and metaphysical theology, a reasonable synthesis of empirical religious knowledge and with implications of critically established values."[34] We have combined parts I and II in our effort to present Macintosh's theory of religious knowledge. It remains to articulate his findings about God and the Divine Economy.

CHAPTER VII

A CRITICAL REALIST'S DIVINITY

An adequate theory of religious knowledge gives us only the basis on which to comprehend the divine order and economy. What we know for sure includes not just what we ourselves perceive clearly and measure. We can also logically project inferable possibilities. There is thus a realm of real possibilities. And this realm includes the biologicaly possible, as well as the logically inferable. Even inanimate physical nature in both the gross physical and sub-atomic spheres has shown us astounding developments, and all within the laws of nature. While, therefore, a critical realist must be cautious about what he regards as so, he must admit that there are more things in the heavens and on earth than most people have dreamed of, and that there is a place, therefore, for "permissible over-beliefs" that go beyond that which is factually and logically demonstrable, but does not conflict with it.

A superlative example of such an over-belief is Macintosh's own argument for a God of the finest and highest living values. He stated this argument in his Taylor Lectures in 1925 and published it in his <u>Reasonableness of Christianity</u>. Before presenting it, however, let us review the process by which he arrives at his conception of God.

He, himself, began his systematic inquiry by tabulating what he considered the relevant data. I recall his listing in class sixteen points concerning God. There were:

1) Reality, not just illusion or idea;

2) Yet not a physical thing or the aggregate of physical things, and not a human person nor the aggregate of persons (and things);

3) The dependable factor responding to the right religious adjustment;

4) The ideal companion of the inner life with whom we may have religious fellowship;

5) Absolute ideal value, including spiritual value insofar as it is imminent in human life;

6) Grace and saving power through Jesus and variously through other persons;

7) The spirit of the group in its cooperation for realization of the ideal, as a "kingdom" and otherwise;

8) The supreme factor of our ultimate absolute dependency;

9) That on which we depend more specifically for the conservation of our absolute values;

10) The creative first cause;

11) The imminent cause of cosmic change; the energy from which all things proceed;

12) The nisus in emergent evolution;

13) The holy in the original fearsome and later moral senses; the <u>mysterium tremendums</u> that elicits our profound awe and deference;

14) The imminent yet transcendent spirit of the universe;

15) The traditional trinity; and

16) The God of historically revealed and discovered attributes; omnipresence, immutability, unchanging righteousness,

absolute love, etc.[1]

But how can one proceed to use these guiding ideas to build an assured understanding of God? Macintosh's discussion of theological method, we have found, proceeds from a basis in an experimental science of religion that yields laws of responses to religious adjustment. Philosophically, however, we are entitled to go beyond such a science to otherwise justifiable hypotheses, just so long as these do not conflict with established evidence or with each other. We can, for example, through imaginative intuition project the hypothesis that God is a value producing factor in the universe.

> "Working in and through the cosmos [indeed], there have been personality creating activities [that are other than human] (cf Shailer Mathews <u>The Growth of the Idea of God</u>, Macmillan, 1931) which antedate all activities of human personalities themselves, and there have been and still are processes and a factor or factors in the education of personalities toward valid ideals, which cannot be identified simply and exclusively with the human. Divinely functioning reality has caused human personality with its immeasurably great potential values to emerge, and through experience is educating humanity toward the knowledge, appreciation and choice of permanently valid values. This divinely functioning cosmic reality, this qualitatively and functionally divine factor we may call God, provided it be understood that, for the present, no further connotation of the term is implied than such as is involved in the foregoing. With this intentionally meager connotation of the term God, it may be affirmed as known fact that God exists. In other words, there is a divinely functioning reality, not to be identified exclusively with the human, and not to be identified with reality as a whole, since not all reality is making for the

> realization of absolutely valid ideals.
> Empirical awareness of this divinely func-
> tioning reality we may call religious percep-
> tion or religio-empirical intuition. It
> seems desirable, for the sake of the many who
> in our day find themselves seriously ques-
> tioning the reality of God in the full
> theistic sense of the word, to enter in this
> way upon a gradual constructive procedure."²

Yet there are what we have a right to consider divine values.

Personality and other values may, moreover, be regarded as Divine. "[R]ationality, beauty and goodness of personal life, individual and social . . . we may reasonably regard as valid ends always [and] everywhere for all persons" and may, therefore, be characterized as eternal and absolute ideals, or values, and not in any altogether static use of these terms." "We may reasonably believe," in consequence, that they will "always be entitled to our absolute or wholehearted allegiance and devotion. Such absolute and eternal ideals or values are, <u>qualitatively</u> considered divine."³

It is at this point that Macintosh's argument in Chapter III of the <u>Reasonableness of Christianity</u> has its clearest relevance. There, concerned with religion at its best for life at its best, he asks the question, What basic attitude is required for life at its best? His answer to this question is, "Moral optimism." He distinguishes moral optimism not only from moral pessimism but also from William James' meliorism which asserted that we have a fighting chance to make the world and life better. Moral optimism is the firm conviction that the values we advance will be sustained, including those of our characters and conscious personalities. This is the faith that enables us to live morally and spiritually, and it involves a cosmic supporter and conserver of higher values, together with the postulate of the responsible agency of man. Moral optimism thus affords moral assurance not only of God, freedom, and immortality but of the universal God of purest righteousness, perfect love, and all other ideal values. This is the God man needs.[4] The cogency of his argument is purely pragmatic. It would not meet Mac's own criticisms of other arguments. It is, as Bixler said, an evidence of great faith--an "over-belief" that has its justification in the quality of life it engenders. It may well serve, indeed, as an hypothesis on the basis of which to build up our understanding of God. One may be able to say, in consequence, as Macintosh does in The Problem of Religious Knowledge that "Divine reality is a reality that [not only] responds to the right religious adjustment [but] that answers prayer . . . regenerates the human spirit . . . maintains the regenerate life . . . promotes the health of spiritual life and develops essentially Christian ethico-religious character." This "same Divine Reality convicts of sin, gives peace and joy, and 'sheds abroad the love of God' in human hearts,"[5] and the faith that he is the kind of God who is characterized by all eternal ideals.

Much has been made in popular religion of the glory of God. I do not recall Macintosh ever using that phrase but for me he has shed very significant light upon it. Some scriptural usages seem to treat it in terms of the glitter of despotic monarchies (and at the expense of their subjects). Even Solomon's glory is suggestive of this, while the streets of gold in the book of

Revelation if not taken symbolically, are reflections of the same conception. But the glory, and the lilies of the field bespeak a glory that quite surpasses Solomon's. The earth is full of his majesty, grace, and creative power. But by far the greater glory of God declares itself in the personal and historic experiences of the love of God, expressed in the forgiveness of sin offered in religion, but also the mountain peaks of highest values to which religion at its best not only asks us to look up and seek with all our powers. The commitment of many people to the finest ideals and principles bespeaks a greater glory for God than any gold or gems or raiment could possibly portray. The "suffering servants" of God, are articulators of the love of God and spokesmen for his perfection. That some persons are overawed by their visions of God is not, therefore, at all surprising.

It is part of God's perfections, and hence of his glory, that he is equally concerned for all persons, even though his providence may generally seem to favor those who observe and meet the requirements of a good life. Yet, it is part of the eternal problem of evil that catastrophes happen to good, and often godly, people. The Jobs of the world's history are evidence of this. There are a very substantial number of victims of circumstance. And such victimization happens within an orderly universe in which religious persons celebrate the faithfulness of God. Both biological processes and external circumstances may amass congestions. The genes of the fathers are visited upon their children and succeeding generations may develop diverse kinds of imbalance, while in impersonal nature, the generous givings of God, as Jesus illustrated in the parable of the sower, may not only be wasted on barren soil, but become glutted with the "listings" of the winds. God does not interfere with the workings of the laws of nature, but uses them to teach men, women, and children the conditions of good, approvable ways of living; the components of a satisfying life.

What then of miraculous deliverances and events of which the scriptures have many? It is interesting that some people seem to stake their religion on signs and wonders--rather indiscriminately--while others view the marvelous developments in nature and human life as revealing the amazing possibilities within a highly ordered world; and, as expressions of the dependableness and constancy of God. This latter was quite evidently the case with Macintosh.

My recollections of his discussions are confirmed by his treatment of miracles in conection with the theologies of Karl Barth, Georg Wobbermin, and Ernest Troeltsch in his last major work in philosophy of religion: The Problem of Religious Knowledge. Barth was a contemporary of Macintosh and was very deeply affected by Germany's defeat in World War I. His theology, in fact, was an "after effect" of that war. The defeat of Germany brought pessimism in the axis nations. Spengler's Decline of the West was one expression of it. Barth's irrational theology was an attempt to counter that deep pessimism. Against a backround of Kantian epistemological dualism it assumes a God of whom humans have, and can have, no knowledge. There can be a revelation of God for those who can exercise faith. But faith is a miracle of God. One must be selected or elected to have this gift. "Hell bent for election" may, indeed, be a crude expression but it seems an appropriate characterization of Macintosh's view of this "miracle." "The difficulty with regard to his doctrine of the miraculousness of faith," he wrote, "is not primarily the difficulty of squaring it with the working principles of science, but rather, its obvious contradiction of the Christian faith in the impartiality and reasonableness of God. It is not that the ideas of divine grace and divine creativity are objectionable, either religiously or philosophically or even from a sufficiently self-critical scientific point of view. What is objectionable from all three points of view is what Troeltsch called an exclusive supernaturalism, according to which God, purely of his own arbitrary will, works miracles of revelation and faith for some and not for others. We have no criterion for detecting such miracles scientifically; we should want no miraculous interventions to bestow favors exclusively upon an elect few; and if we must hold that creative intervention is God's way, or one of God's ways of counteracting or eradicating evil in the world, our scientific, religious and philosophical interests combine to support the surmise that experience will show such divinely functioning creativity to be universally dependent upon the existence or fulfillment of certain definite condtions, natural or human."[6]

Macintosh's conclusions are further shown in his treatment of the theologies of Wobbermin and Troeltsch. The former, Macintosh wrote, has written much that shows "great insight and wisdom" with "definite potential . . . for constructive theology," even "for those who do not fully share his epistemological presuppositions." "He is on strong ground," indeed, in "holding to the idea of the Kingdom of God while rejecting apocalypticism; in emphasizing the divine power of Jesus to save the world while dismissing the virgin birth story as inessential; in retaining the idea of miracle in the sense of direct experience of the immediate activity of God, as distinct from scriptural marvels that are not acceptable to science and historical criticism [or scholarship]. . . . He thus holds to the finality and validity of Christianity as the religion of redemption. . . . "[7]

About Troeltsch with whose theology he found basic difficulties, he, nevertheless, wrote, "This means then that the one true miracle which can be experienced by every man is revelation--not enlightenment merely, but the experience of the life of God in regenerating, liberating, uplifting the human soul."[8]

In his own "resultant doctrine of God," in his Normative Theology, Macintosh is cautious about using the word miracle in connection with revelation. "We must not assume that man . . . has no responsibilty for the [emergence in him or] exercise of religious faith. The fact is that at two points man's free activity, responding to the divine initiative is called for. In the first place, man must enter as fully as he can into the right religious adjustment. When he does so, and . . . begins perceptibly to reap the experiential benefits which tend dependably to follow, there will tend to emerge within his consciousness an imaginal intuition to the effect that the God we imperatively need actually exists, a God supremely trustworthy and worshipful, fully adequate in character for all our religious needs." Macintosh cites instances in which this has occurred, then "the second point at which man's free participation in the genesis of faith is called for is the need for man to affirm, as fully as he critically and conscientiously can, in thought and life, the truth of the religious intuition which has thus emerged. . . . In this way he transforms what might otherwise be a passing intuition into an abiding faith."[9]

Add, therefore, to the constancy and astounding resources of God the human affirmations in the sacrificial services of the suffering servants of world history, the devotion to highest standards and values that are vested in God by billions of persons over many centuries, the joyous choirs of earth and joyous other modes of devotion that acclaim God's love and perfection, and we have a spiritual glory of which the purest gold and finest raiment are but the meagerest of symbols. All this, despite his non-use of the phraseology of the "glory of God" is very much more than implicit in Macintosh's religious philosophy.

He writes in summation in <u>Religious Realism</u>,

> "And so, it is surmised and comes to be affirmed in the name of religion in its higher, more ethical and spirtiual develop- ments not only that the religious object, God, to whom adjustment is made, is spiri- tual, characterized by ideal moral goodness,

spiritual beauty and rationality, and that he is the main objective source of spiritual progress insofar as this is manifested as a result of religious attitudes and experience, but that the spiritual everywhere is divine in quality, and this for the reason and in the sense that it is rooted in the being and nature of God. Thus a religious interpretation of the cosmic process in which these presumably divine values are produced is suggested. Not only is the divine object to which religion adjusts itself affirmed, on the basis of successful religious adjustment, as an existent reality and as being at work in man's spiritual progress and reality called God and the laws and energy of the physical world--a relation which, it is felt, may be somewhat analogous to the relation between the human mind or spirit and the human body."[10]

"This analogy [in fact] of the physical organism and its imminent intelligent life I should like to enforce by means of a parable which I have used in my classes and which, I find, is similar to an illustration used by Professor Boodin in his suggestive article entitled 'God' in the Hibbert Journal for July 1929. Let us, for the sake of our parable, take panpsychism seriously and suppose that electrons really are conscious. And let us stretch the theory to include the supposition that normally these conscious electrons are intelligent and good observers, and that some of them have received a modern scientific and philosophical education. We can imagine a metaphysically-minded but realistic and somewhat sceptical electron speculating as to the nature of man. The physical man would be to him a complex galaxy in which molecules and atoms would be comparable to our solar system and worlds. They would be separated by such vast distances, from the electron's point of view, that it would seem fantastic to suppose that the whole human galaxy was a living organism controlled by a central intelligent mind. Man's inner conscious life would not be an externally observable fact. All that could be directly observed by the scientific electron would be certain fundamental processes, apparently quite mechanical, and, within the human cosmos broadly considered, a process of growth and a more or less dependable behavior. These might be interpreted by vitalistic electrons as indicating some super-mechanical principle, an entelechy directing the growth and a psychoid controlling the behavior; but even such theories would be regarded by many as ultrametaphysical and going beyond the observable facts. Processes working toward recognizable ends would be pointed out, and it would be admitted that such processes were quasi-teleological, that is, <u>as if</u> they were the expression of conscious purpose; but it would be thought unscientific to imagine that they really were consciously purposive. Even in connection with the habitual modes of behavior it would be possible to point out, as an ingredient, certain eternal mathematical forms; and, in order to refer to this ingression of the eternal objects of reason into the flux of events, some mathematical and philosophically minded electron with a flair for introducing new terms into the vocabularly of philosophy might invent the name, Principle of Concretion; but while it might be deemed permissible to apply to this rather abstract Principle of Concretion some such symbolical term as Mansoul, it would be with the explicit understanding that in reality the principle of concretion, Mansoul in its primordial aspect, while ideally perfect, was not only not conscious but even deficient in actuality. And so the philosophical electrons might go on discussing endlessly the metaphysical nature of the human organism, and hesitating to attribute conscious mind to man for fear of being charged with projecting into the human galaxy their own sublimated libido. But whatever certain psychologist electrons might think of such 'phantasy-thinking,' it would be true all the while that man <u>is</u> intelligent mind and will expressing itself through his bodily behavior.

"We human beings in relation to the universe are like these imaginary electrons in relation to man. We can discover a principle of concretion, the ingression of eternal objects into the flux of events, and processes working toward ends <u>as if</u> they were consciously purposive; and yet all we can observe directly is cosmic behavior; we are never able to observe from without the inner

> life of any supposed cosmic or divine mind.
> But if there were such a mind, the situation
> for us would be just what it now is. Perhaps
> there is, after all, a central mind and will
> in the universe."

Macintosh's "perhaps" here is not one of doubt but of nondogmatism.[12]

CHAPTER VIII

VALUATION AND SOCIAL REALISMS

I began this essay with Macintosh's search for a philosophy to guide us through imprecise and diverging traditions and personal experiences. It was Macintosh who in this way "awakened me from my dogmatic slumber." Simeon Spidle, with whom I had had five semesters of philosophy at Acadia University, had not quite succeeded in doing this. Spidle was a notably clear teacher, however, whom I used to consult on academic and intellectual matters--even calling at his home or telephoning him (Mrs. Spidle sometimes mistook my voice for that of President Patterson, and coming to the phone Spidle would say, "Yes, Dr. Patterson").

Spidle, indeed, developed an openness in his students through his balanced presentation of both sides of an issue. And, while on occasion he would state his reasons for what he regarded as the best (Christian) position, he left it characteristically to his students to think matters through for themselves. The more conservative Baptists were not favorable to this degree of openness, though a story current in my student days showed some sense of humor. Spidle used to spend his summers in southern Nova Scotia, and while the local minister had his vacation Spidle preached in his church. The Deacons, one summer, approached him about preaching a sermon on Hell. All their other ministers, they said, had done this. Spidle consented, and in his sermon explained various views that had been held about Hell. "Now ladies and gentlemen," he is reported to have said in conclusion, "you may take your choice."

Spidle's chief limitation was that he had every philosophical position too neatly packaged, and did not so much arouse queries as give alternative answers to questions other philosophers had raised. The mootness of the issues, with their relevances to current human concerns, was not adequately evidenced.

Not so with Macintosh. His philosophical queries arose out of downright human concerns that he had coped with, and he led his students in a studied and intensively informed way through the byways and by the dead ends of proposed answers to human predicaments.

His was a physical, as well as cultural, world. He was at once idealistic, in the moral and spiritual sense, and pragmatically yet critically realistic, in the personal and social sense. One gained from him a strong sense of the comparative relevances and irrelevances of different philosophies and of both the basic and far reaching importance of philosophy as such for the depth and level of life. Concerned with human living at its best, he did not become stymied in a maze of incidentals.

Religion was the milieu for the highest and most basic human commitments, and, as we have seen in Chapter VI, it was no inclusively valid matter. There were poor and, even, bad religions, and the determination of the grounds of religion at its best was an issue not for conservativism or liberalism but for philosophical comprehension.

Labelled by William S. Harbaugh, in an early draft of his biography of John W. Davis, as "an old school Baptist by inheritance and upbringing, and conviction,"[1] his Chicago experience with G.B. Foster and others had taught him that "there is nothing in the past that belongs to the past alone,"[2] that devotion to ideals is fundamental in religion, yet that religion must be harmonized with science, and given adequate foundation in philosophy. It will then become not only sound religion but the necessary inspirer and bulwark of the good, and, indeed, the best life. Such a religion he thought of in basically orthodox terms, as requiring God, freedom, immortality, the mediatorial work of Christ (to which a virgin birth was not essential but undoubtedly a relic of an ascetic conception of matter and sex). Yet, his procedure was quite untraditional. Hence, the title of his theological autobiography, "Toward a New Untraditional Orthodoxy."[3] That a critical, monistic experimental realism in religion should issue in an orthodoxy, however untraditional, disclosed the philosophical possibilities in historical religion, and a faith that can survive quite honest doubts.

Macintosh taught me, indeed, that philosophical thinking must, in its very nature, be independent: always evaluating traditions, along with scientific findings, and one's own experience in the world of values and disvalues, together with envisaged possibilities that can be rationally tested. Meaning literally "love of wisdom," philosophy is love not simply of knowledge or of intellectual vision but of achieved understanding that fully satisfies the mind as well as the "heart."

Macintosh found that the pragmatisms, idealisms, and dualistic realisms did not do this. Hence, his development of a critical monistic realism. From him I thereby gained the concept of an overall realism: in value theory, ethics, social philosophy, and religion, as well as in epistoemlogy. Having already dealt with both his epistemological and religious realisms, it remains to treat his moral, axiological, and social realisms.

With his Chicago orientation, human ideals and other values were fundamental to Macintosh. Defining value in some contrast to R.B. Perry's "general interest theory," as anything that contributes to a teleological process, he did not conceive of all such processes constructively. Hence, he recognized both end values and end disvalues, as well as instrumental values and evils. End values include not merely such goals of processes as character, fulfilled personality, and an ideal kingdom or society of ends, but likewise the contemplative values of science, philosophy, art, and religion, and the associational values of companionship, collaboration, social organization and interplay. All such ends are known partly at least by appreciative intuition, but the feedback from men's approximations to these ends discloses wholesomeness or unwholesomeness in objectives and engrossments. Euphoria, for instance, when it neutralizes concern for other values, is an end that is open to question, while other ends may be found to cost life's finer and even basic values.[4]

Macintosh followed Walter G. Everett[5] in distinguishing eight kinds of human value: moral, social, esthetic, hygienic (i.e. bodily), ecomonic, political, religious, and intellectual (e.g. scientific, philosophical, reflective). The first seven, Macintosh says, are values for life; the eighth he regarded as value for knowledge (and wisdom). But knowledge is a component of life. Thus, values for knowledge are special values for life. That they are frequently ends-in-themselves does not distinguish them from either esthetic or religious values.

Each of the main types of value has instrumental value for the other types. Morality, for instance, has value for health, society, religion, knowledge, good government, responsible industy and commerce, and wholesome art. Social values are of primary importance in morals, economics, politics, and also, significantly, in hygiene, religion, aesthetics, and knowledge. Aesthetic values, in turn, reach into mental health, business, religion, intellectual inquiry, and of course, politics. Political and economic values have been both overstressed and understressed. There is no doubt, however, of their essential importances for living and of their outreach into every department of living. Likewise, the effects of science are very difficult to delimit, while philosophy, often seeming so hazy and abstruse, concerns our basic ideas, or what W.E. Hocking termed our "stem ideas" in every sphere of thought and life, undergirding whatever faith we maintain and casting the vistas which illumine our lives. As for religious values, these were Macintosh's special concern. We shall try, therefore, to summarize his thought about them.

Religion has had, and still has, effects through all of life. Its impacts on morals, personal psychology, health, art, politics, society, science, philosophy, education, etc., have been so well recorded that discussions may seem needless. But the cases have been stated both excessively and deficiently--sometimes, indeed, quite negatively. Christian scientists have treated it as the only essential condition of health, while others have emphasized the instances in which its practices have interfered with or militated against health. Likewise with morality, many have thought of religion as the only basis of morals. Others, in and out of turn, have envisaged religion as conducive to irresponsibility and even immorality (in the cases of fanatics and zealots), hence interfering with a really humane morality. As for the social impact of religion, historical theocracies, as in Puritan New England, articulate one conception of its role, while Marxists, conceiving religion as the opiate of the people, have been endeavoring to produce a society without it. (That in the process they have developed another religion, with a substitute God of a cosmically materialistic dialectic process, has been overlooked.) Economics is a product of communally political organization for Marxism, while Tawney's <u>Religion and the Rise of Capitalism</u> has shown a case for religions, like that of the Puritans, of industry and thrift.[6]

We could continue this tabulation for art and knowledge, maintaining both that the only sort of art that is worthwhile is religious or that the only real knowledge is that of religious revelation, and that religion hampers both art and knowledge. But a constructive statement would distinguish the effects of different kinds of religion and, notably, of religions which emphasize moral and other ideal values (fundamental religions Macintosh called them) along with religions which stress relationship or adjustment to a supreme cosmic power who or which may be quite variously conceived. When conceived in both personal and moral terms, this Power, for Macintosh, has strengthening, cleansing, and enriching effects on character, health, artistic creativity and appreciation, social relations, political perspective and activity, economic well-being, scientific and philosophical orientation. All of this can be historically documented and experimentally tested. Religion can thus be a tremendous enricher and transformer of life, while its value in itself as vision and communion bespeaks a spiritual sublimity that cannot be adquately captured in literature or art but which in moral religon feeds back into character and joyous services.

What Roy Wood Sellars called "justified endorsements" of the contributions of things to the processes in human life and culture[7] is also, for Macintosh, the validation of values. His ethics, or moral philosophy, follows from his philosophy of values and may thus be called an axiological ethics. He assesses the elements of truth in the chief types of ethical theory: intuitionist, rationalistic (as in Kant), teleological or empirical (hedonist, utilitarian, pragmatic, self-realizationist). Morality, he finds must be rational in the sense of reasonable, not _a priori_. It must be concerned with the consequences of action, yet sensitive to intuitions, particularly regarding ends which may, in turn, be progressively tested. It must be the expression of free conscientious intelligence and hence spiritual rather than purely hedonistic. "It is better" indeed, as Mill phrased it, "to be a man dissatisfied than a pig satisfied." Nor is happiness in its broader, deeper sense the sole motive. It would be wrong to sacrifice all other values to happiness. Not that the fulfillment of life is not the greatest value, but that its achievement at the expense of the fulfillment of others would be dubiously moral. The fulfillment of self, in the sense of the gaining of the finest range of values, in conjunction with the fulfillment of others, is the moral standard. And this, for Macintosh, involves a rigor of principle aproaching Kant's ethics, together with a sensitivity to the interests of others, reflectively governing a concern with the consequences of courses of action. Above all, it involves a good will.

In his classroom Macintosh listed six active constituents of the good will, including:

1) The will to be an admirable person oneself, in the sense of an admirable character;

2) The will to serve humanity with especial reference to the higher values;

3) The will to be rational in conduct, elevating the more important considerations above those of less import, and so organizing one's living;

4) The will to power (or strength) in moral action;

5) The will to use the sources of moral power;

6) The will to the satisfaction of human desires as these fit into the rationally moral organization of life.

Macintosh's Valuational Realism is not, therefore, a Platonic or Hartmannian axiological realism, although one at least of his statements might seem quite like it. "I hold," he wrote in the Preface to The Problem of Religious Knowledge, "that there are absolute values, universally and eternally valid for persons, which values (or ideals) we can progressively learn to appreciate and realize [and] that reality is whatever it is for there to be such valid values and for their realization to be imperative."[8] Yet Macintosh's valuational realism is a functionally critical realism for which values disclose themselves as confirmable goals and means of human living. Their adequacy to a desirable quality of life, and especially to an adequately fulfilled life, is their validation. Their neglect or misuse means at least a deprivation. They are thus basic, intrinsic components and conditions of living in our type of world.

Macintosh's functionally critical realism also extends to his social philosophy. He did not write or lecture on social philosophy per se, but a social philosophy is implicit in his writing and teaching. And his reasoned efforts toward citizenship assumed it. He was certainly not a social realist in the sense of those who view individuals simply as products of and subsidiaries to society. Nor did he have a social emphasis like that of John Dewey. He was more clearly an individualist than Dewey seemed in his philosophy. Individuals have ways of making themselves, for Macintosh. But individuals gravitate toward association, and, to serve their common interests, constitute themselves as groups with policies, practices, and norms. They institute mechanisms for advancing and safeguarding their interest. So nation-states come into existence in social evolution, and churches and denominations. Families, of course, are basic groups, though less well-organized in modern times, and yet, variously supported by other groups. And families have grown historically into clans and tribes, and tribes into nations, and nations into nation-states, with systems of government, commerce, communication, education, transportation, health, recreation, welfare, and, quite notably, defense. The evidently natural proliferation of social groups, along with the basic services they provide or facilitate, is witness to their reality.

Macintosh is a moral idealist, as well as a functional realist, in his social philosophy. The concept of a kingdom or society of ends (a kingdom of God) has its grounding in a real, natural (and hence physical) world, and a critical realism will discriminate these potentialities. What we said, therefore, about Macintosh's view of moral values applies also to social values. Moral values are basically social and social values are or should be moral, as both end and instrumental values. They lend themselves, indeed, to statements of principle in terms of moral rights and wrongs, goods and bads. The best life for all, however, is not necessarily an ideal life for any, but the ideal life for each (in his social relationships) is a normative or regulative idea that should point to our social endeavors.

Although Macintosh did not write philosophical treatises in social philosophy he did write on social issues. Take for instance his writings on "Disarmament"[9] and "War." His letter to the Editor of the Chicaco publication Unity, in 1932, concerning "War," is worth republishing here because of its clarifications:

"Editor of Unity:

> In your signed article entitled, 'Unbind the Conscience of the People', in your January 18th issue, along with many statements with which I can heartily agree, you assert that I will never oppose another war, that I have offered no theoretical objections to war as such, that in any future war that seems to me equally justified with the recent World War I will be willing to kill as many of my fellowmen as my bayonet and bombs can reach, and that my case has consequently no moral value.
>
> Will you kindly take your readers into your confidence, Mr. Editor, and let us all know just how you have secured this seemingly supernatural information? It may be, as you intimate, that I am not very 'clear cut' in my thinking, and, if that be the case, probably that is why I cannot see that you have the right to conclude so much as to what I would do from my careful minimum statement of what I would not do.
>
> I find on consulting my records that in a statement written in June 1929, for the information of the Judge of the United States District Court at New Haven I said,
>
>> I am not certain that under no possible circumstances would I support a defensive war. (By what logic can this be made to mean that I would support any future so-called

'defensive war?') At the same time I am very strongly of the opinion that no events are likely to occur within my lifetime such as would justify a declaration of war on the part of the United States of America. Moreover, I am in agreement with the best judgment of well-informed persons that any major war in the future would be so absolutely disastrous to the human race that it is scarcely possible to exaggerate the importance of our doing everything that can reasonably be done now to secure the future peace of the world. To this end it has seemed to me that full freedom to oppose unjustified war is of the first importance.

I have repeatedly said I would support any war I would regard as morally justified, but would not you, Mr. Editor, support a war if you believed it to be morally justified? Have I ever in recent years named any specific war which I could regard as morally justified? I have repeatedly pointed out the distinction between a just cause and a just cause <u>for war</u>. It does not follow, because China has just cause for complaining against Japan, that she is or would be morally justified in going to war with that country. A war may be morally unjustified for any one of variety of reasons. (1) its cause may be in itself unjust; or (2) while its cause may be just, all other possible ways of securing justice may not have been exhausted; or (3) it may be improbable that justice will be secured by having recourse to war; or (4) it may be better to suffer many an injustice than to cause the injustice and other evils that would be involved, incidentally, in going to war.

While the World War was on I did believe that Great Britain and Canada had been morally justified in entering the war on behalf of France and Belgium, and that the United States was morally justified, in view of the Allies' refusal to consider 'peace without victory,' in going into the war to bring the war to an end more speedily and at the same time secure the future freedom and peace of the world. But why should it be supposed that I can have learned nothing since 1918? As a matter of fact, while I am no historian I am of the opinion that weighty reasons may be found for doubting whether the Unites States has been morally justified in going to war, not only in the Mexican War, but in any one of her six historic wars. The cause of 'no taxation without representation' was a just cause but is it certain that the American colonists could not have secured it since 1776? America may have had cause for dissatisfaction with England in 1812, but did that justify morally the invasion of Canada, and did the war settle the matter in dispute? It was not even mentioned in the treaty of peace. There undoubtedly was ground for dissatisfaction with the rule of Spain and Cuba and the destruction of the Maine was a great shock to the American people; but we now know that Spain offered to arbitrate everything, and one is tempted to compare the action of the United States in that instance with the action of Austria toward Serbia in precipitating war after the assassinations at Sarajevo. This leaves the Civil War and the World War to be considered. Are we quite certain that the abolition of slavery could not have been achieved, as it was achieved in many other countries, without recourse to war? And can we be sure that, if Colonel House had not made to the Allies certain conditional predictions or virtual promises of American assistance, they would not have turned a more favorable ear to President Wilson's appeal for 'peace without victory?'

In short, had the principles now formulated for us in the Briand- Kellogg Pact been followed by this nation, in the months preceding each of its historic wars, I am not sure but that every one of those wars might have been happily avoided. And with this thought in mind I am free to repeat what I have said before, that I think it extremely improbable that there will arise within my lifetime circumstances under which the United States would be morally justified in declaring war.

Why then do I not become an absolute or unconditional pacifist? Why do I hesitate to say that never under any possible circumstances would I support the use of armed force? Perhaps you would say, Mr. Editor, that if I were more 'clear-cut' in my thinking, I should know more, and that if I knew more, I should be an absolute pacifist. Something like that does seem to be the trouble. I feel that <u>I don't know enough</u> about the future and its possibilities <u>to be an absolute pacifist</u>. It seems to me that just as the use of physical force by our police may under certain possible circumstances be justified, so there may arise circumstances which would justify the use of military or naval force for national or international police purposes. I am inclined to think that when the fundamentally pacifistic Ramsey MacDonald sent British troops to Palestine to keep the Arabs from slaughtering the relatively defenseless Jews, he was morally justified in so doing. And I cannot be sure that a similar situation, in which the use of armed force would be morally justified, might not occur again.

It will be hard enough presumably, when the time for decision comes, to tell what we ought to do; it is still more difficult to make an intelligent absolute promise so far ahead of time and without any exact knowledge of the actual situation we may have to confront. We can, of course, express beforehand the principle to which we give our allegiance and to which we may hope we will have courage enough to be faithful when the time for action comes. One can promise to be guided by whatever may seem to be, when the time comes, for the highest well-being, not of one's own nation alone, but of humanity in general, or of everyone, likely to be affected by the consequences of one's action. This I did not refuse to do. I said I was willing to pledge allegiance to the United States, but not with the understanding that in doing so I was promising readiness, in my future obedience to any future American government, to act against conscience, the will of God, or the highest welfare of the world.

I cannot but feel, Mr. Editor, that it is not universally valid moral principle, but a rather doctrinaire pacifism, which leads you

>   to say of my position on this matter that it
>   'has no moral value.'
>
>   Douglas C. Macintosh"[10]

The Editor's footnote, quoted next, shows the dogmatism that tended to beset the unconditional Pacifists of those days. He wrote:

> (Note: Professor Macintosh honors UNITY with this very full and clear statement of his position on war, written in a spirit of courtesy and good will which should be a model to us all. It is our feeling, however, that what he writes, elaborately confirms our original statement. . . .)

The Editor's original statement included the phrasing that in any War that Macintosh considered as morally justified as he had considered World War I he would be willing to kill as many of his fellowmen as his bayonet and his bombs could reach. Presumably this statement was intended as symbolic rather than literal since as a purportedly responsible Editor, he must have known that Macintosh had served as a Chaplain in both the Canadian and American armies, and did not kill anyone. By what logic, indeed, he can, on the basis of Macintosh's well-reasoned statement of facts and principles, conclude that the letter "elaborately confirms our original statement" is difficult to comprehend. It was certainly not Aristotelian or Hegelian, or even Symbolic (in any intelligible sense). He seems simply concerned to reassert a dogmatic, unconditional, ultra-Pacifism.

Macintosh's position, <u>per contra</u>, is that of a balanced, realistically moral, yet profoundly religious man of highest ideals and loyalties.

Macintosh also wrote late articles on "Our Crime Problem" and "After Prohibition and Repeal, What?"[11] The article on the crime problem is a quite different type of study for Macintosh: A broadbased statistical study of methods for dealing with criminals: Its philosophical element is simply its statement of principles: The protection of society and of the criminal himself, together with his rehabilitation. He needs above all to be treated with understanding and friendship as a distinctive person.

Macintosh had become especially concerned with the issue of crime through the influence of Miss Genevieve Cowles, an artist who painted a religious picture for the walls of the state prison at Wethersfield, CT, and "brought about the setting up of libraries in various jails," obtaining many good books by her personal solicitation. She also secured competent speakers to conduct forums in the jails. She herself made frequent visits to the county prisons, befriending the prisoners both during their imprisonment and after their release." She interviewed judges and others in positions of official authority about a melioration of conditions in the prisons, and "finally, she . . . sought to convey to others her own enthusiasm for the cause." The article, therefore, tells at least as much about Macintosh's humane responsiveness as it does about his social philosophy.

Similarly, Macintosh's volume on Social Religion published in 1939, is an expression of his will to participate in social decisions. Having been rejected for American citizenship, he still wished to cast votes. He undertakes to do so in a written elaboration of principles. The principles he enunciates are unqualifiedly Christian. The moral idealism of the original social message of Jesus is unequivocal, and Macintosh quotes his Chicago Professor G.B. Foster that "Jesus is not behind us but before us" and "only those who strive for a better life can understand him."[12] Macintosh does not deny that Jesus is behind as well as before us. Two statements from page 366 of The Problem of Religious Knowledge (PRK), in fact, support the view that Jesus is before us because he was behind us. The first is that "in character and spirit, in attitude toward God and man, in the spirituality of his personality, and in the inspiring and redemptive function of what he did for others, Jesus of Nazareth represented [and hence represents], we may well believe, not only humanity at its best but the highest human embodiment in history of those absolute values or spiritual ideals which we have designated as divine." And from "the point of view of its significance for the race and for religious thought, there is no revelation to compare with that which we find in the historic Jesus as the Son of God, or Christ of faith. In his divinely holy and loving spirit we find our best and only satisfying norm of the divine as imminent in the human and as also 'in Heaven,' [i.e.] in the realm of reality that transcends the scene of our earthly experience." Though historically, indeed, "we may remain in serious doubt as to to the historicity of particular sayings attributed to him, we can be almost as sure as we could wish to be about the kind of person he was, what his attitude was toward God, and toward his fellowmen, and what in its spiritual and social essence his gospel was."[13] He quotes such erudite biblical scholars as B.W. Bacon, F.C. Porter, George Cross, M. Dibelias, Karl Holl, and E.F. Scott in support of this conclusion.

The key to the social teachings of Jesus, he points out, is to be found in the "second Isaiah."[14] For him the coming of the Kingdom of God was good news--in contrast to that of the stern preaching of John the Baptist and other exponents of divine wrath. When the "sons of thunder" expressed a "wish that a thunderbolt might destroy" some hateful samaritans, "the master's rebuke was immediate and conclusive." He must, indeed, "have tried to make it clear to his followers that they should show a different spirit from that of Elijah; they must not be destroyers of men, but their saviors (Lu 9:52-56). They must learn to bless those who curse them, to do good to their enemies, and even to love them (MT 5:44). . ."[15] Jesus' gospel is literally one of good news; it is glad tidings to the poor, the afflicted and oppressed, and concern for the well-being, the adequacy of life, for all. It is a gospel of righteousness, peace, and active good will in human relationships.

The Kingdom of God is basically an inner, non-political kingdom. It is something within the heart, mind, and will of individual people that issues in qualities of character and service expressive of a relationship to the perfect Father--and in no sense an arbitrary, much less despotic, Being. Such a relationship can only be articulated in acts of unselfish love toward one and all. Its spirit and outreach are stateable in terms of a new commandment that goes beyond the technicalities of conformity to moral laws by including them as essential ingredients in inspired human services. "That ye love one another as I have loved you" follows the gleam of pure personal concern for people.

The ethical perspective of the Kingdom of God is one of moral perfections, "Absolute honesty, absolute purity, absolute unselfishness, absolute love. . . . These ethical standards are all to be found in . . . the fifth chapter of Matthew. . . .[16] Be ye therefore perfect" is the injunction, and it is not simply directional. Nothing less than absolute purity in absolute love is adequate. "As rock salt exposed to the weather would lose its saltiness and be useless to preserve anything from decay, so must the followers of Jesus be careful not to lose their honesty, purity and unselfish love if they are to keep society from corruption and destruction." Only thus can they be the "nucleus of the growing Kingdom of heaven on earth"[17] and bring the greatest values into human life. It is not just for the sake of the perfections that one is to achieve them, but for the quality of life they engender. We validate ideal values by the "joy" they give to life, and service for the quality of life that all may have is the motive of the Christian. Doing unto others as you would have them do to you is an ambiguous standard unless one has such a humanly moral ideal. Doing as you would have others do to you could be selfishly bilateral. But "if a person has a true estimate of values so that what he is seeking is the [great living values of the] Kingdom of God . . . then and perhaps then only can he [rightly] do for others what he would have others do for him."[18]

It seems redundant to say that the Kingdom of God is social. Yet some kingdoms are dubiously so if that which is social is moral. A cruelly oppressive social system or one sustained by fraud is certainly not moral. That, in turn, which is moral is, charactically, social, in the sense that morality bespeaks an impartial viewpoint on the behavior and treatment of persons and groups. The Kingdom of God is a Kingdom of special concern: For God and man. It is not an imposed Kingdom. It is surely not one that comes on "the clouds of heaven," with or without great shouting, as some people still want to envisage the "second coming" of Christ.[19] It issues, we repeat, from within, and issues in a society of actively good wills, sharing in the abundance of possible values. It is a democratic society, "so democratic (indeed) that people would be justified or condemned according to their attitude toward the seemingly most insignificant member. . . ."[20] Distinctions of rank, insofar as they obtain at all, are distinctions in humble service. That the "Kingdom" calls for intelligent service and not just the indulgence of loved ones or of one's own sympathies is implicit in Jesus' teachings. It is for the joy and not the later grief of those served.

Jesus' principles advocate a new society in the sense of one transformingly renewed through spiritualy generated individuals. To think of it as a brotherhood of man has become hackneyed. To regard it as a family of God may make it appear too unworldly. But the practice of the imminence in life of spiritually ideal values and of their expression of a creatively divine Father spells a good life into which people everywhere may enter and share. This, indeed, is not characteristically good news for those who place primary emphasis on worldly possessions, nor for those who are much concerned with social status. The "Kingdom of God" is not a class or caste society, and, of course, it is not a communist one--in the Marxist sense. Is it communistic in any other sense?

The early church was communistically motivated for a brief period, but discovered that an undiscriminating communism was self-defeating. How, then, practice the giving up of worldly possessions and maximum concern for the good of others? Are Jesus injunctions here just regulative? Or are they unrealistic? They are certainly a matter of principle.

The communism he espoused was, says Macintosh, "the ideal communism of brotherly love." That it is not intended to be indiscriminate is shown in Jesus' response to Zaccheus, "who was congratulated on having experienced emancipation . . . even though what he promised to give to the poor was only _half_ of his goods, in addition to restoring fourfold all that he was conscious of having fraudulently exacted." To 'give to him who asks of you and turn not away him who would borrow from you' "must be interpreted with the grain of salt of common sense. But that does not mean regarding them as maxims of an interim ethics . . . mistakenly imposed under the influence of a false expectation . . . what we have here is a graphic illustrative statement of an ethical ideal eternally and universally valid, namely willingness to share so fully with others that ultimately all will have what they need for the most effective use of their powers for the greatest good of the human race." And it does presuppose the conditions under which this may be so, and in any case, "<u>it is always morally imperative that we come as close as is possible</u> under the circumstances <u>to the ultimate ideal</u>."[21] Our second principles should clearly envision and be the nearest possible approximations to our ideal values.

Macintosh might seem sentimentally unrealistic in his perfectionism or moral idealism. Actually, as we have stated, he approaches Kant in the rigor of his commitment to principle. That in his <u>Reasonableness of Christianity</u> he should encompass 133 pages before treating the historic Jesus was, he wrote, "no oversight." "There is an important tactical advantage in showing how extensive and vital is that content or essence of Christianity which can be defended without any assumption as to particular facts of history. We escape the dangers of infecting the entire content of essential Christian belief with the necessary incertitude of historical opinion." And we put value as a dominant factor in universal processes. This, in fact, is also the most assured disclosure of qualified opinion regarding the historic Christ who "exalted purity of heart, inwardness, humility, childlike sincerity, courage, freedom from covetousness, generous forgiveness, love of enemies, <u>unworried trust in God as the perfect Father</u>, unselfish love and service to the poor and needy and to the outcast and little children" (Italics added).[22] This much historic knowledge we have with scholarly certitude, and it is knowledge of the role of value and principles of value that Jesus found to accord with cosmic order.

Does this perfectionist religious idealism of Macintosh accord as neatly with his philosophically critical realism as he seemed to hold? He, himself, distinguished Normative Theology, based on ideal values, from Empirical Theology, concerned with dependable responses to religious adjustments together with intuitional leads toward further personal comprehensions. He also distinguished both of these theologies from Metaphysical Theology which undertakes to cope with ultimate questions of divine reality: e.g., the relations of the natural and supernatural, the immanent and the transcendent, time and eternity, the relative and the absolute, God as both one and three, the real and the ideal.

Normative Theology, indeed, is a projection of Empirical Theology. The God of Empirical Theology guides "the religiously surrendered will to right decisions and actions," promotes "sensitiveness to sin, the peace of reconciliation, and unselfish love of God and man." The "divinely functioning reality who does this for man is a morally redemptive God, man's ethical savior and friend."[23] That we are thus "furnished with a norm for an intuitional Normative Theology," from the God of complete, ideal righteousness is readily envisaged, above all, in view of the perfectionist ethics of Jesus.

For religious metaphysics, in turn, on the question of divine imminence contrary to the one-sided supenaturalisms, on the one hand, and the purely mundane humanists, on the other, Macintosh had no difficulty in envisaging God as both imminent and transcendent. As suggested in Chapter VII, he found a clue to God's imminence in the world in the relation of the human mind and spirit to the human body and its world. If it thus be admitted, he wrote, that God's relation to the physical universe could be like that of the human mind to its physical organism "the question arises as to whether it is only in the physical realm, the realm of the lower values, that the divine, the absolutely worthful, is to be regarded as imminent and revealed, and not also in even so God-like a human personality and life as that of the historic Jesus. In general, then, in spite of the very unfinished state of metaphysical thinking on this subject, it would seem that the analogy of the psychophysical organism promises to throw some much needed light upon the problem of imminence and transcendence in its theological aspects."[24]

The relation of ideal standards to their often poor, human approximations then becomes intelligible, the natural shades into the supernatural--and conversely, and the doctrine of the trinity is an expression of God's creativities in both the human world and that of transcendent values.

This God of transcendent, ideal values, moreover, is not the God of more primitive conceptions who predestines some to moral evil or to purely arbitrary election. A "morally perfect God would not be willing that any should ultimately perish. Neither would our Normative Theology admit any such partiality in God as would, apart from any essential differences in the instances, work a miracle to help one individual and decline to do the same for another. Furthermore . . . we can take another step and deny that disasters to human values which often comes through the orderly operation of the habitual processes of nature are to be interpreted as being in themselves the expression of the creative will of God at the time."[25] A God of morally perfect love wills the greatest good of each and all, provides circumstances for self-redemption, and raises all vistas to the very highest best.

Macintosh concludes his Metaphysical Theology with the statement:

> "We have gone but a very little way into the problems of metaphysics in which religion and theology are interested, but far enough, perhaps, to justify the suggestion that it is the special task of theological metaphysics to hew out from the quarry of available fact and truth and give at least rough general shape to building stones which may be used in constructing the temple of metaphysical theology. In the latter discipline direct attack has to be made on the problem or problems or a reasonable philosophical interpretation of such fundamental theological concepts as God, revelation, Christology, salvation, providence (including theodicy), and immorality. It is thus the function of theology in metaphysics to suggest new problems and give a new tang to old problems, and to make contributions not only to the content but possibly also to the certainty of metaphysics. On the other hand it is the

> function of metaphysics to give a more reasonably defensible content (by way of both addition and subtraction) and a more rational certainty to theology. Theology and metaphysics have done each other much harm from time to time in the past; but that was largely because of the faulty methods employed by the one or the other, or by both. But for the best results in either field, given the use of the right method on both sides, theology and metaphysics are mutually indispensable.
>
> "It is not, however, the lot of the epistemological Moses to enter into the promised land of metaphysical theology, but only to lead the philosophical pilgrim to a place where he can from a distance 'view the landscape o'er'."[26]

But Douglas Macintosh saw through the mental eyes of many more seers than Moses, and seems to have understood the meanings of their visions.

CHAPTER IX

RESPONSES TO CRITICS

I quoted in our Preface Reinhold Niebuhr's quip at Mac's sixtieth birthday dinner that his next book should be entitled "My Students and Other Battle Lines." The Festschrift to which eleven of his eminent students contributed essays would seem to give evidence of this, though their deep respect for an indebtedness to him also obtrudes. Before presenting these genial, if variously penetrating, critics, however, I must mention some others who come within my personal experience. I recall, specifically, Liston Pope who had succeeded Jerome Davis as Professor of Social Ethics and later became Dean of Yale Divinity School, saying in the early forties--after reviewing Mac's <u>Social Religion</u> not so favorably--that Macintosh's social philosophy seemed to be an old-fashioned, now discarded, liberalism. Since epistemology and philosophy of religion were Mac's fields, however, and not social philosophy, and since he wrote on social religion mainly to gather up some strands of his life and thought, Pope's criticisms seem incidental and only incidentally relevant.

A mere pertinent criticism came from a Vanderbilt graduate student who had spent a year taking Macintosh's philosphical courses at Yale. He had gone there with a background of philosophical idealism and was evidently looking for vulnerabilities in Macintosh's epistemology. He was, in fact, writing his doctoral thesis on the Macintosh philosophy, and in that thesis he contended that the latter's conception of "perception-in-a-complex" was dualistic epistemologicaly, rather than monistic, that the object of experience and the actual thing (or situation) which it was thought to designate were not the same. I shall delay my evaluation of this criticism until I relate Macintosh to Roy Wood Sellars with whom he had notable affinitives yet sharp divergences.

There were, of course, philosophical critics right at Yale, and at times bitterness seemed to enter into their relations with Macintosh. He recounts, indeed, in his statement of the development of his theology ("Toward a New Untraditional Orthodoxy") from <u>Contemporary American Theology</u> in 1932, that coming to Yale from the Chicago school of pragmatists he was not warmly welcomed by more pnilosophical members of the school.[1] He, nonetheless, established himself at Yale, while including a pragmatic element in a developing realism. Yet, gaining stature philosophicaly brought its oppositions. I recall from my own years at Yale, 1925-29, the evidently bitter opposition of some members of the graduate department of philosophy to the work of two of Macintosh's graduate students who had written doctoral dissertations on philosophical questions. There was an interlocking relationship between the graduate departments of philosophy and religion, and members of the philosophy department who were interested in the philosophical theses or graduate students in Religion were invited to share in the oral examination on these theses. I remember one mature and competent student who, much to Mac's chagrin, was denied his doctorate through the efforts of one member of the philosophical faculty. I also recall the instance of a candidate in my own doctoral group with a thesis on the theory of freedom in the philsophies of Renouvier and others. He came out of the examination looking very pale. That sparked me for my examination on "Pantheism in Neo-Hegelian Thought." So when Professor C.M. Bakewell surprised me with the question, "Have you ever experienced a devil?" and I was not sure whether I was confronted with one then and there, I responded, "Sometimes I think I do."

Professors Bakewell and (C.A.) Bennett were said to be the "enfants terrible" of the doctoral examinations. Bakewell, actually gave me no trouble. How I responded to his query whether Jesus' use of the analogy of the vine and its branches was a pantheistic statement, I do not recall. It was certainly not a memorable answer. And all I remember of his criticism of Macintosh's philosophy per se is that he was opposed to his realism and ontological dualism. Bakewell was a non-theistic pluratistic idealist, whereas Macintosh following an early period of addiction to absolute idealism, had become a sharp critic of all versions of idealism. We have dealt with Macintosh's critique of Bakewell in Chapter IX.

As for C.A. Bennett, whose <u>Philosphical Study of Mysticism</u> Macintosh referred to from time to time, the opposition seems to have been or quite different sort. Having been in one of Bennett's courses briefly--until dropping out to have more time for my thesis--I gained the impression that Bennett's criticism of Macintosh was less philosophical than pedagogical, that Mac's students seemed to reflect attitudes such as Bixler expressed in one of the quotations from him in my Preface: that to listen to the "absorbing clarity" of his position was to have the feeling of "really penetrating to the essence of the subject. 'This is it' we used to say to ourselves as we heard him." Yet Bixler himself had long since demonstrated the independence of thought that Mac generated in his students. It was the earlier response to Macintosh's teaching, however, that Bennett seemed to find hampering. Yet, that is apt to be a circumstance attending any great teacher.

More meritorious were the criticisms of his variously distinguished former students. Macintosh responded to these in three essays in The Review of Religion in 1939. The first was a response on behalf of empirical theology, and addressed especially to the essays of George Thomas, Vergilius Ferm, and J.S. Bixler.[2] (The second essay was directed to "Theology, Valuational, and Existential," Bixler again getting exposure for a one-sided valuational conception of religion, but more especially Richard Niebuhr's existential stress on the irrational component in religion. The third dealt with Rheinhold Niebuhr's claim that religious statements are mythological.)

Thomas has offered a critique of Macintosh's scientific empiricism in religion, on the one hand, and his argument from moral and other value considerations to supplement his findings from experimental religion, thereby claiming a reasoned faith. Neither method, Thomas elaborated, accomplishes what Macintosh maintains. An experimentally empirical basis for theology assumes, first of all, a dependable connection between the right religious adjustment and the right response, but different religions have different conceptions of both the right adjustment and the right response. The attempt to establish a divine source for the response to religious adjustment must also fail. An inference to such source is not, in fact, scientific but philosophical and the conclusion is preferential rather than firmly demonstrative. Scientific evidence yields only proximate not ultimate causes. And whatever, indeed, may be said for critical realism's "perception-in-a-complex," it has dubious value when applied to religious perception. Such direct experience might tell us that God is, if we already had adequate differentia by which to identify him, but that means by unscientific preconception. Macintosh's use of moral considerations, moreover, to establish a personal, ideal God assumes a relationship between value and nature, and an organic relationship between man and nature. Certainty about this, however, is unattainable and Thomas thought it "downright insincere to stake one's life on an hypothesis."[3]

Mac's response to Thomas involves his response to others also. Ferm and Bixler likewise contend that religion has no cognitive value. We shall treat Ferm and Bixler momentarily, but first his response to Thomas. He had admitted ten years earlier in one of my classes, the criticism that his <u>Theology as Empirical Science</u> was flawed by assimilating historical Jewish-Christian religion into experimental data and by "laws" which were philosophical rather than scientific. Yet, he stood by his position that religion had a basic experimental component and could in principle be scientific.

"Now," he writes, "it seems to me a very serious objection to make against religion that it has, and can have, no cognitive value. From the beginning religion has been practical and experimental adjustment and not contemplation merely. The history of religion may [indeed] be regarded as a prolonged 'trial and error' process aimed at finding out just what religion is experimentally good for" and so "what kinds of religious adjustment are dependably effective. . . . It seems impossible [therefore] to separate the question of the practical value of experimental religion from that of its value for knowledge. Religious beliefs [in fact] are not forever to be treated as merely plausible." A commitment is involved, and this commitment, in turn, may open up new evidence that might not otherwise come to one's attention. When, moreover, Dr. Thomas maintains that we can rationally justify our intuition of a cosmic purpose only by means of a philosophy of nature and man, "I would point out that partial verification of a divinely functioning teleological factor may be found in the experience of development toward a universally valid ideal of moral character and spiritual personality, with the help of reality's response to a persistant cultivation of a certain discoverable, dependably effective religious adjustment."[4]

As for the question of what constitutes a right religious adjustment, we can judge that by its "effectiveness in tending to produce in the human will, and in the resulting behavior and experience, effects which are qualitatively in accord with divine, or absolute, ideals." And similarly with "establishing a _divine_ source of the response to man's adjustment," the finding may in principle be scientific.[5]

The rejection, additionally, by both Vergilius Ferm and J.S. Bixler of an empirical theology is associated in both instances with a theology and view of religion that is open to serious criticism. "Dr. Ferm seems to have no criterion to apply to religion," and so far as his essay is concerned, "his essay is a mere project, not a _fait accompli_. His religion without theology is blind feeling; his theology without religious experience is [in Kantian parlance] an empty concept."[6] It would strengthen Dr. Ferm's philosophy of religion, nonetheless, were he, "instead of defining the religious object as whatever is taken as being of 'serious and ultimate concern' he would define it as that which is seriously felt to be of ultimate concern."

Bixler's position gets much fuller treatment at this point and substantial further treatment in Macintosh's response in his essay on "Theology, Valuational and Existential." His high esteem for Macintosh has been presented in my Preface. Yet, Macintosh points out that he accepted only one of the two tap roots of religion that Macintosh had disclosed on the basis of extensive studies. It was the valuational nature and function of religion that Bixler accepted, not its belief in a real deity as the source of both existence and value. Scientific formulations, Bixler urged, cannot do justice to the ideal values in terms of which theology treats; they cannot solve universal problems of value or answer the question of how the ideal can be realized.

Comparably to his colleague Kirsopp Lake who uses the term God to
refer to immaterial Reality, or "Values," "Truth, Beauty, and
Wisdom," Bixler defines God as, "absolute value, 'an essential
rightness in the realm of truth, beauty, goodness, or in all
three,' 'the holy as the absolute good,' 'a Kingdom of ends,' 'a
realm of intrinsic worths,' 'a world of values,' and object of
thought belonging exclusively in the realm of the <u>Sollen</u>, not in
that of the <u>Müssen</u>, or <u>Sein</u>--in short, not any transcendent Being
but 'the transcendent ideal' with its absolute claim upon us."
His interest in phenomenology shows that he is "interested
apparently only in the pure <u>what</u> of Deity, not in the Deity's
existence." "I do not know," Macintosh continues, "to what
extent this extreme one-sidedness may have been suggested . . .
by my customary insistence that devotion to a Divine Ideal
without belief in the existence of a Divine Being would be
preferable to belief in God's existence without any concern for
obedience to the will of God, or the Divine Ideal. In any case I
would remind him that I have always maintained that conscious and
voluntary relationship to an <u>existent</u> Divine Reality is essential
to religion in the full sense of the word" and that <u>we can have
knowledge</u> of dependable responses to our adjustments to that
divine reality. Bixler's "exclusively valuational theology or
religion whose God is a mere combination of essences will never
meet the practical religious needs of men. It is a truncated
half-religion, providing a worthy ideal as the object of worshipful devotion, but no adequate object of religious dependence and
trust."[7] That Bixler admitted some of the force of Macintosh's

criticisms is indicated in his statement quoted in the Preface that "he could outthink us with one hand behind him, and some of his comments that he wrote in the [three] reviews were devastating." He made an exception in a letter to me in 1979. "I have never been able to understand," he wrote, "why he connected me with Kirsopp Lake. Of course I had read Lake but never felt any affinity."

It is the Niebuhr brothers, Reinhold and Richard, however, who get the fullest use of Macintosh's intellectual scalpel. We have already dealt with Richard's theology of irrational religion (Chapter VI). Macintosh's more rounded use of the data of religion, along with his pointing out the rational assumptions of Richard himself, discloses another instance of emphasis on one element to the exclusion of others. I proceed, therefore, with Mac's response to Reinhold Niebuhr.

Entitled "The Truth in Myths," Reinhold's essay asserts that "the transcendent source of the meaning of life is in such relation to all temporal process that a profound insight into any process or reality yields a glimpse of the reality which is beyond it." But this glimpse is not capable of statement in anything close to literal terms. It can be expressed only in the language of myth. Its terms are the "most adequate symbols of reality because the reality which we experience constantly suggests a center and source of reality which not only transcends immediate experience, but also finally transcends the rational forms and categories by which we seek to apprehend and describe it."

Macintosh states:

"Now, the words I have quoted must have been written fully three years ago, and I have no information as to what Professor Niebuhr has been doing in the Gifford Lectures which he has been delivering this year (1939). I would hope, however, that he has been keeping closer to the terms of Lord Gifford's will than did his recent predecessor, Karl Barth. If so, he will presumably have had a grapple with problems of religious epistemology and theological metaphysics, in which case he may perhaps have been led to correct some of the anomalies of his position. It may even be that he will be found to have returned to something like what he wrote over twelve years ago (<u>Leaves from the Notebook</u>, etc., p. 152), and to have developed more fully at least the opinion which I have quoted once already, that 'there is at the heart of almost every tradition an element of reasonableness and around its circumference a whole series of irrationalities,' and that it is 'our business to destroy the latter and restore the former by fitting it to contemporaneous circumstances and conditions.' This may be wishful thinking on my part, but until I am informed to the contrary I will try to trust, even if only faintly, this larger hope.

Meanwhile I offer some further animadversions on Professor Niebuhr's published opinions on the subject before us, interspersed with a few incidental suggestions of a constructive nature from my own point of view. I would agree, of course, with Mr. Niebuhr that the fundamentalists make a great mistake when they take the primitive, prescientific myths of the Bible story as literally true in either a scientific or a metaphysical sense. We can easily reconcile ourselves, as Christian believers in God, to a permanent place for poetical and 'mythical' elements in the concepts employed in the religious group with which we are associated, provided it be clearly understood that at least the most important theological concepts, such as that of God as a superhuman rational intelligence and moral will, are to be taken as literally true and their contradictories as literally false. But if all our best religious ideas are to be dismissed as more poetic representations of an inaccessible Something which we not only can never begin to know but can never even think about with real and literal truth, the result of finding this out must be fatal, not only for theology, but ultimately for the life of practical religion itself. . . .

As a matter of fact, the main task of the theologian, in one way of stating it, is just this: the distinction and separation of literal truth from all mere figure of speech in the language of religion. We can recognize as symbolic the concepts of Warrior, King, Judge, and even Father, when applied to God; but to deny ultimate theological validity to such terms as spirituality, rationality, purpose, and moral goodness (The Nature of Religious Experience, pp. 119, 131; cf. pp. 100, 102), is to undermine the very cornerstones of religion.

Theology cannot, without fatal loss to religion and life, be reduced to what Niebuhr calls permanent myths. In the name of integrity of the theological conscience and the security of religious faith, protest may well be made against the doctrine that, in religion, one has the right to use as if they were literally true ideas which neither are literally true nor are translatable into terms that have an equivalent meaning and can be taken as literally true. It was not without reason that even [Hans] Vaihinger, not a theologian but a philosopher, refrained for thirty-five years from giving out for publication his ethical and religious functionalism [in his Als Ob]. So far as I can see it, it is only his intense moral earnestness and not anything in his theological mythologism which distinguishes Reinhold Niebhur's philosophical position, fundamentally, from that of the fictionalist, Hans Vaihinger."[8]

Both Reinhold and Richard Niebuhr, in fact, show too much influence of Kantian agnosticism, on the one hand, and German existentialism, on the other, though Reinhold's existentialism is partially at least distilled through Paul Tillich.

I had always thought of Macintosh as primarily a philosopher of religion. His theology certainly was philosophicaly based, and to a notable degree it was philosophicaly articulated. With his chief work in epistemology referred to as a "monumental study," a "classic" in philosophy per se,[9] the philosophical caliber of his professional writing was strongly supported. So far, however, we have dealt with critics who were chiefly theologians. Two eminent philosophers also get comments in Macintosh's responses to his former students. F.C.S. Northrop and W.M. Urban are the two. Northrop had contributed an essay to the Festschrift and had spoken of Macintosh's major epistemological opus as "so fairly" and "systematically" presented, a "classic" in the field. Macintosh responds to Northrop, however, in a single paragraph which I quoted in full:

> "The paper of Professor Northrop, who is a specialist in the philosophy of science, deserves a much more extended and critical review than can be given it here. The somewhat technical discussion leads up to what looks to me like a plea for the authority of a speculative philosophy of science in questions of epistemology, both general and religious. Now, it is a fact that the scientific specialist has, in his own special sphere, a certain expert authority which outsiders do well to recognize; but the same thing cannot be said for the speculative philosopher, even when he is a philosopher of science, and there are certain prominent speculative features of Dr. Northrop's own thought-system which other philosophers of science are very far from finding it necessary to accept. It is true enough, however, that his familiarity with scientific concepts and scientific results tends to gain for him a certain relative authority among thinkers less scientifically informed than himself."[10]

Professor Urban was a colleague of Macintosh at Yale, but not a contributor to essays honoring him. In an article in the Journal of Religion in January 1939, Urban contended that the data or religious perception are non-sensuous for Macintosh, in contrast to their sensuous nature for W.N. Wieman. Macintosh, writing at that time in review of the essays in the anniversary Festshrift, utilized the occasion to respond to Professor Urban. He wrote:

> "This gives me the opportunity of explaining [to Prof. Urban] what I mean by 'perception in a complex,' particularly in relation to religious experience. An equivalent term would be perceptual intuition, both terms being used in a very broad sense. By intuition I mean immediate awareness, not in any such exclusive sense as would necessarily deny all mediating or representational elements, but in the sense that the cognition of truth or of present reality is, or is felt to be, not indirect or tentative, but essentially self-authenticating and direct. Intuition, in this broad definition of the term, may exist in any one of four varieties: rational, appreciative, imaginal and perceptual. The first two have to do with the apprehension of axiomatic truth and intrinsic value, respectively. Imaginal and perceptual intuition differ from each other in that the latter is certitude of truth about reality not presented sufficiently for perception. Imaginal intuition, while frequently fruitful, is notoriously fallible, and even perceptual intuition is sometimes illusory, needing to be tested in further perceptual intuition.
>
> It will be seen that there is nothing in the foregoing definition of intuition which requires the limiting of the application of the term 'perceptual intuition' to the physical. In both the physical and the psychical realm there may be 'perception in a complex.'

We apprehend such physical process as walking, striking and lifting in various complexes of sensory and other elements of experience; and we also apprehend empirically, or perceive, such psychical processes as perceiving, remembering and desiring in various complexes of elemental sensa, revived images and constructs, such as may be distinguished in introspective and behavioristic analysis. Furthermore, it may be maintained that we apprehend, with comparable directness, physical objects in the complexes of physical qualities and processes, and the psychical subject in complexes of psychical processes, such as perceiving, remembering, thinking and willing. It is not necessary to reason that I am because I think. I apprehend myself intuitively in the very process of thinking, feeling and acting which I also apprehend perceptually, whether introspectively or behavioristically or both.

"Essentially the same things may be said with reference to religious experience and what it enables us to apprehend. There is an element of appreciative intuition involved in the marking off of valid religious content from other contents of the experienced. Religious value is a complex category, including the objectively valid spiritual ideal (e.g., the absolutely good and true) as well as the subjectively numinous (at least potentially). But the apprehension of divine reality involves not only the appreciation of holiness, divineness; it involves also the empirical intuition or perception of actual process and participating existential cause, whether this be interpreted ultimately in subjective or objective terms, whether as many or one, and whether as personal, impersonal or superpersonal. Perhaps this may serve to indicate what I mean by perception of divine reality in the complex or religious experience."[11]

We turn now to a more thorough-going test of Macintosh's philosophy. At the beginning of the chapter, I mentioned the Vanderbilt student who contended in his doctoral dissertation that Macintosh was actually an epistemological dualist rather than the monist he purported to be. To take account of this and the wider range of specifically philosophical criticisms that we cannot undertake to encompass, I shall simply relate Macintosh to Roy Wood Sellars whose kinship with and divergences from Macintosh are striking. Their kinship was personal as well as philosophical. Both were born in Ontario, Canada, Macintosh in 1877, Sellars in 1880. Both studied in America: Sellars at the University of Michigan, Hartford Seminary, the Universities of Wisconsin and Chicago; Macintosh at Chicago, following a bachelor's degree at McMaster University (then in Toronto). Both were also involved in affairs of conscience: Macintosh's case was epochal as I have indicated in Preface 1. It concerned the issue of promising to bear arms in defense of the USA regardless of the justice of the war. Sellars' revolved around his early Fabian type of socialism.

Philosophically, they shared similar forms of critical realism and ranked 1 and 2 chronologically in the development of this epistemological position. Sellars had given inklings of it in 1908 and 1909 and had completed a volume under the caption of <u>Critical Realism</u> by 1913--though it was not published until 1916. Macintosh, meantime, had given intimations of realism in an article on representative pragmatism in 1912,[12] stated it explicitly in 1913,[13] and incorporated the conception into his monumental <u>Problem of Knowledge</u> in 1915.[14] Though independently derived, the conceptions of critical realism were quite similar. Both start from the common sense realism of every day experience and modify it on the basis of the attested findings of science.

Both formulate a monistic theory of perceptual knowledge, Macintosh maintaining the position consistently from the start while Sellars was only incipiently an epistemological monist in his earlier years--developing that position, indeed, with most clarity and effectiveness in the late fifties.

The parallels between Macintosh's and Sellars' philosophies extend, moreover, to their levels of knowledge, emergent cosmologies, organicisms, problems like freedom versus determinism, and their philosophies of value.

It is in their theories of perceptual knowledge and their organicisms that I find significant supplementary differences. Macintosh had elaborated his position most fully in an anthology on <u>Religious Realism</u> in 1931.[15] The substance of it was that the human body is in real spacetime and its sense data, as in pain, are real indicators not only of locus of their stimulation but as clues to its source. Evolutionary development and racial history have both contributed to the specializations of the sense organs and brain functions that make them effective in locating and distinguishing the stimulating factors. By the process which Mac labelled "perception-in-a-complex" we can also demark the nature and function of things per se, i.e., in a complex of sensing, remembering, reasoning, and sometimes imagining, we identify stimulus objects which, in turn, are in a complex of things and circumstances. We identify not only physical entities in the external world but "animal life, consciousness, the self, other selves, physical activities, and more or less complex processes and relationships, physical and psychical, individual and social."[16] All are instances of "empirical intuition . . . or perception-in-a-complex, a direct, non-inferential awareness of the reality and presence of physical" and transphysical entities or processes.

It is on this point that the Vanderbilt student contended that Macintosh's critical realism was dualistic. "Perception-in-a-complex," he contended, is based on sense data which are, therefore, the objects we immediately perceive. And, if it be argued that we perceive <u>by means</u> of sense data, then our perception is indirect and hence dualistic. But as Sellars wrote in <u>Contemporary American Philosophy</u>, we see through our sense data to the object, somewhat as we see through a window--and the window is not the object of perception until some condition such as mist or dirt calls our attention specificially to it.[17] It is here, moreover, that Sellars later pinpoints what Macintosh was saying. Sellars had objected to the use of the term intuition to indicate the basic mode of perceptual knowledge. Intuition for him was an immediate awareness of colors, sounds and other sense elements as such and not the awareness of the objects of these data disclosure. Yet Sellars uses a similar concept to Macintosh's perception-in-a-complex when in his ethics he recognizes with the deontologists, an immediate, though not independent, rightness of certain acts.[18] His criticism, therefore, of Mac's assimilation of insight into intuition is largely one of semantics. Sellars, in fact, is so much in agreement with Macintosh that he really makes more explicit and better documented what had actually been maintained by Macintosh. That we perceive real things, and not just sensations, or sense data, Sellars points out, is confirmed by "feedback" from the stimulus objects, sensations are thus shown to be signs of objects beyond themselves, and guides to things. We see beyond the sensation to the impinging thing and are thereby able to discriminate fearsome or desirable objects and situations often with immediacy. The complexity of the process is no more a denial of <u>direct</u> perception than is the complexity of the human eye.[19]

Perceptual knowing is, of course, only one mode, or level of knowing, though it is included in such complicated levels as those of atomic and astrophysics. The distinction between implicative and perceptual knowing is common to Macintosh and Sellars. Macintosh labels the former "mediate knowledge," and the latter "knowledge by acquaintance." The conceptual elements in the former are dominant, and in the latter recessive, while assisting perceptual identifications. Scientific perception, for instance, may involve an extensive background, and hence "apperceptive masses."

Other areas of kinship between Macintosh and Sellars include, as I have mentioned, their theories of freedom, values, ethics, and conceptions of the universe. Sketching the first three of these briefly, Macintosh's findings concerning freedom grew out of his study of the literature of the problem of freedom versus determinism, and bespeak a "somewhat creative synthesis of Bergson and T.H. Green." In his 1911 Oxford lectures on the perception of change, Bergson mantained that the ultimate unit of change is always itself a changing, and not a series of static components. Applying this to the character of thinking, willing self that, as Green said, determines which desire should motivate his action, that character is in its reflective choosing in process of coming to be and not simply an after effect of its conduct but as a determiner of further conduct and the making of a creative choice.[20]

Sellars characterizes such development as that of "agential causality" and gives it a neurological basis. "At the brain-mind level," he wrote, "we enter a region of creative adjustment and exploration dominated by needs and a job to do." Integrative activity, giving rise to action as a whole, with patterned growths becoming coupled with other patterned growths, and spontaneity combining with reflective thought respond to a "need for adequacy of adjustment."[21] The emergence of human beings' great brain thus gives rise to a self-guiding type of causality that (contra the transeunt and imminent types) uses reason and expresses free will. A person becomes an agent and not simply an instrument of a process.

As for ethics and the theory of human values, the respective positions of Macintosh and Sellars grow out of their conceptions of people's agential capacity for responsibility. Values, Sellars holds, are functions of things in the lives of persons and groups. Such functions need not be explicitly valued, though the validity of conscious valuations is a primary issue. True value, or adequate evaluation, concerns the justifiability of the assigned value of any role which anything may have in human life. There is often much delicacy in working this out. Feelings of approval are involved, but also--and more importantly--judgments (involving conceptions and, of course, language) regarding the relevance of things to human needs and wishes, together with the merits of the ends or objectives that humans at least implicitly acknowledge. "We must learn to discover how events, objects, plans, patterns of human living fit into our lives."[22] The emotivists and intuitionists have not fairly glimpsed this problem. But Toulmin's stress on good reasons for moral judgments, and Hare's careful study of moral language have opened a way between intuitionism and emotivism, with a "recognition of an interplay between criteria and attitude" in evaluation. Yet the clarification of valuational reasons needs much better development.

This elaboration accords with Macintosh's conception of value as anything that contributes to a telelogical process, and with his type of teleological ethics for which the fulfillment of the self is the moral standard. There is feedback from the valuational activities that evidences the sufficiency with which valuations fit their objective--and its connection with satisfactory human living. Reasons are adduced for both normative and instrumental values, and the reasons are supported by postulates and data that must be respectively testable. The conception of a good life, in terms of the finest range of values, is involved, together with that of a good society serving the fulfillment of persons. Justified endorsements that service such a life is for Macintosh, as well as Sellars, essential in the validation of values. There is, I repeat, there is a rigorism on Macintosh's ethics that approaches that of Immanuel Kant, but in both Macintosh and Sellars there is much more downright sensitivity to the interests of persons than in Kant.

Sellars is more systematically a moral philosopher, publishing four essays in ethics *per se*, along with some dozen others on values more generally. The outcome of his ethical inquiries is a combination of utilitarianism with deontology that recognizes the immediate, though not independent, rightness of certain acts.[23] Sellars' ethics is more strongly social in orientation than that of Macintosh, so much so, if fact, that prior to the social legislation in U.S.A. in the 1930's, Sellars was a Fabian type of socialist. That legislation disclosed the possibilities for an essentially moral capitalistic democracy.

I shall delay the question of kinship in organicisms for the concluding question of Sellars' and Macintosh's complementation of each other. Despite their notable kinships, however, they diverge diametrically in ontology, the mind-body relationship, and the philosophy of religion. Sellars was an emergent materialist who conceived of matter as actively dynamic, instrinsically endurant, relational, and self-organizing, capable of producing such marvelous emergents as the great human brain together with the whole range of valuings that can make life profoundly satisfying. Macintosh, per contra, was an emergent metaphysical dualist for whom survival of the conscious soul was a basic factor. The duality of mind and brain was crucial to him, whereas for Sellars, the distinctivity of the human brain lies in its being a minded brain that observes, thinks, feels, coordinates and controls activity, and is itself guided by ideas, purposes, elaborations of plans, reflective choices, and commitments.[24] The basic difference in their views of mind, in fact, that is for Macintosh mind (as soul) is eternally endurant whereas for Sellars it is matter that survives physical death, not as brain or body but simply as rudimentary matter.

It is in their philosophies of religion, in consequence, that one would expect their divergence to display itself most sharply and there it does disclose itself unmistakeably. Not that Sellars was an irreligious philosopher. He had a year, in fact, at the Hartford Theological Seminary, and he had written volumes on religion in 1917 (<u>The Next Step in Religion</u>) and 1928 (<u>Religion Coming of Age</u>). In the early thirties, he drafted the <u>Humanist Manifesto</u> which was signed by John Dewey, Eustace Hayden, E.S. Ames and some thirty others, then published in <u>The New Humanist</u> (1933). This was followed by papers on naturalistic humanism in the 1940's and a critique of religious existentialism in the 1960s. Sellars was, in fact, one of the earliest of the twentieth century American humanists and a spearhead of that movement.

"I see no evidence that the Universe is deiform" ("replete with purpose and plan"), he wrote in "Naturalistic Humanism."[25] The tremendous potencies that emerge with marvelous structure among which the human brain stands far out are offset by the terrific waste in cosmic trial-and-error. The universe itself is creative. It is endlessly engaged in integrations and disintegrations from which emerge occasional novel entities that perpetuate and modify their species. But the universe is not God in the sense of a perfect, conscious Being. Yet, this is no reason why man should not think and live in terms of the most meaningful life. The very concept of the spiritual should include health, wholeness, appreciation of the finest values, concern for others, and the richest human relationships. Yes, man is *in* nature. Nature is his home and area of life and competence. Let the artist and the poet speak out here. Even music and language are inseparable from vibrations. And yet, man is himself--not a *part* merely but--an agent, dreamer, chooser, and thinker. Let the existentialism of Kierkegaard be enlarged and made realistic. . . . A cosmic and a planetary view, a social view and an intrinsically personal view: these must be woven into a well-evidenced and constantly tested perspective."[26] The vast riches of the universe and life will yield the religious experiences of wonder and awe, and one will, indeed, ask himself why is there anything at all in existence rather than sheer nothingness.[27] This will intensify and deepen his consciousness of human values.

Yet, all this would make Macintosh react as he did to Eustace Haydon's *Quest of the Ages* which he reviewed for *The Humanist* in January 1930. Macintosh wrote:

> "The author's acquaintance with the facts of religion, historical and contemporary, is ample (except, possibly at one point), to qualify him, at least so far as empirical information is concerned, for his chosen task of formulating a philosophy of religion. . . . But I have been repeatedly reminded while reading the book of the old fable of the fox that had lost his tail in a

> trap. To make the best of a bad matter . . .
> he called an assembly of all the foxes of his
> acquaintance, and after a long harangue on
> the unprofitableness, of tails in general and
> of a fox's tail in particular, he proposed
> that they all follow his example and have
> their tails amputated, thus adopting the new
> fashion which was so very agreeable and
> becoming."[28]

The illustration, however, seems unfortunate, as though ontological religion were a tag-end. For even if tails are vestigial to some, they are of integral importance to others. What Macintosh really intends to say is, of course, that Haydon's religion has a superficiality about it because of the omission of something most basically essential. In point of fact, he regards it as quite onesided, though largely right in its affirmations.

Macintosh, indeed, criticizes H.E. Fosdick for stating that the humanist must be a cynic with respect to the values he espouses. The humanist, writes Macintosh, is "not logically required to be cynical as to the supreme worth of the life lived, as long as it does last, for friendship, beauty, truth, and that greatest of all goods, the good will."[29] What Macintosh calls "fundamental religion" *is* humanistic. Religion, indeed, which is not humanistic is not the religion of Jesus. But "fundamental religion" is only part of the story. A very basic half of it is omitted, and Macintosh refers to those who treat it as the whole of religion as "pitiably mutilated Christians." Yet, note that he calls them Christians, though they miss out on the personal values of adjustment to a cosmically supreme personal Power.

> It is true enough that if we could not have in our lives both the pursuit of truth, beauty, and goodness, and a belief in God and immortality, but had to choose between them, and if we were certain that one could and would continue adequately to pursue the highest values as well without as with those religious beliefs, we should be justified in choosing the pursuit of spiritual values rather than an empty theological belief; but, of course, this is not the true state of affairs. There are many for whom it is possible, psychologically as well as logically, to choose not one or the other of the suggested alternatives but both. . . . They feel [moreover] that they have the right to believe as they ought, if they can and they are glad to find that, in all scientific open-mindedness, they can."[30]

Macintosh's argument for the existence of the God of Christian ideals is, in fact, a form of the argument from human values which in his essay on "Experimental Realism in Religion" he finds permissible scientifically, epistemologically, and cosmologically.[31]

The cogency of Macintosh's argument is a different matter. In an article in the <u>Readers Digest</u> on "Is There a Substitute for God?", Journalist David Klein thinks to gain cogency by combining the argument from the human need for a basis of self and social control with the argument from the Bible.[32] There, indeed, is a rub! The assumption that nature itself is without creativity and controls ignores the amazing designs produced by natural processes as in the stalactite formations in caves, the majesty of great mountains, the terrifically long evolutionary processes of the eye, life histories of great animals, not to mention the dew drop and the waterfall. Yet, malformations that do not survive must also be acknowledged and evolutionary dead ends. But as

Sellars asks, Why is there anything whatever in existence?[33] And the patterning process in nature, why is it operative, together with the conditions for the emergence of new kinds of existence? Macintosh could, indeed, with biblical support, have viewed God as an experimenter in creation. The Genesis account relates that after creating light "God saw that it was good." Likewise after creating dry land, herbs and growing things, the stellar systems, and living organisms: God saw that each and all were "very good." But man--and woman--soon began to present a problem. At times he was far from good and grossly in need of salvation. Hence the emergence of the Christian gospel. Man, Macintosh found, needs a cosmic God of ideal values. He found that to be so in his life. He saw it in the lives of thousands of others, and found it experimentally confirmed as well as bolstered by innumerable evidences.

For Macintosh <u>God is in the creative process</u> despite all deviations. There is, indeed, creativity, and basis for morality and lofty values, and providence at least within systems, and faith that bestirs religious adjustment and yields spiritual strength and solace. And these bespeak an alternative that goes quite beyond humanism. Here, therefore, is a basic divergence of Macintosh from Sellars.

Can it be said that each still fills out the other? In certain respects, this is so. Sellars's vigorous intellectual honesty, for which he paid a price, ignores the human need for a personal living God or whatever equivalent there could possibly be. And that there is a basis in matter for the realities and high values that it is able to generate, Sellars elaborates but does not account for. Hence Macintosh has something to offer not only psychologically, but also anthropologically. Sellars' scientific grounding, on the other hand, could have made Macintosh more rigorously discriminating, on the one hand, and scientifically more advanced and documented, on the other. Sellars' documentation of the emergence of life, the brain-mind relationship, and the nature of perception provide models that enabled me to present him as a thinker who had crossed "philosophical divides."[34]

Earlier I mentioned organicism as an area in which there is agreement between him and Macintosh along with supplementing divergence. Compare Sellar's statement in the anthology on A.N. Whitehead with Macintosh's broadly sketched, imaginative comparison of our relation to the universe with that of an electron's relationship to man. "We human beings in relation to the universe," he wrote, are like "imaginary electrons in relation to man. We can discover a principle of concretion, the ingression of eternal objects into the flux of events, and processes working towards ends *as if* they were consciously purposive; and yet all we observe directly is cosmic behavior; we are never able to observe from without the inner life of any supposed divine mind. But if there were such a mind, the situation would be for us just what it is now."[35]

Sellars' organicism is less imaginary. He wrote:

> As an emergent evolutionist working on a realistic basis, I have been led to stress

> organization and integration as ontological facts, and therefore to reject eleatic materialism of the billiard ball type. But this meant to me not a plunge into subjectivism [as taken by Whitehead] but a basic challenge to extreme atomism, that togetherness in nature meant a synthesis in which components entered into new and intimate relations such that a genuinely novel unity emerged with characteristic capacities and properties. I was led to think of an emergent causality, transitional between transeunt and imminent causality [whereas for Whitehead causality is basically imminent . . . creative of a new and different substance.
>
> Now the curious implication of this emphasis upon [natural] organization is that it seems to me that mine is more a philosophy of organism than is Professor Whitehead's. In the microscopic cross section of the contemporary world of actual occasions, he is an atomist, even though these actual occasions participate in a common past. I, on the other hand, as a reformed substantialist, hold that there are co-existent substances expressive of different levels of evolution which are the scenes of transeunt, emergent, and imminent causality."[36]

A position which comes close to combining Sellars' scientific realism with Macintosh's intellectually articulated realistic religious faith was espouses by J.E. Boodin. In a Functional Realism he held that "things exist only in fields, in mutuality with other things, and that they have properties only in their dynamic interrelations." "To understand the creative advance in nature," he states, "we must have more than just a succession of stages."

> It is impossible to understand how nature can be measured everywhere into the same units without some control which is not that of the units themselves. Nor can we understand the architecture of nature that repeats itself in the atoms and molecules and

> molar masses of matter when the conditions
> are similar. We can only understand such
> similarity of architecture when we conceive
> the cosmos as the architecture of pervasive
> genius . . . [and] we conceive the cosmic
> genius as a nisus which guides the process
> onward, and beyond the further levels, but it
> must not be something in the future [as in
> Samuel Alexander's view] but a present actu-
> ality in order to be the guiding field of the
> advance.^{37}

This does not mean that there is no refractoriness in nature; there is much of it. But Boodin thinks that the "principle of cosmic laziness is a sufficient explanation for the tardiness and refractoriness of nature."^{38} Man's own deviations result additionally from the factors of impulsive wishing, scheming, and choosing. At every stage, in fact, "there are the possibilities of individual initiative according to the capacity of the individual and the conditions in which he finds himself. . . . [And at] every stage there is the call to advance, the stimulus to new organization, to a new creativeness; and at every stage advance is conditioned upon the willingness and capacity of individuals. . . ."^{39}

The "genius of the whole" operates to create new spiritual, along with other, patterns, including the needs of men for relationship with the Spirit of the Cosmos. Macintosh could have said that. Indeed, he published it in his anthology on <u>Religious Realism</u>. Such a venture of intellectual faith, while going beyond what can be clearly demonstrated, is not only a permissible overbelief; it pragmatically enlarges the lives of many people. Here again we have a Macintoshean type of answer to his critics--and an assured escape from the wilderness of modern thought.

CHAPTER X

THE MACINTOSH BEQUEST

What is the enduring status of the Macintosh personality and achievements? The notable memories will have totally disappeared in another generation or, at the very most, two. The Fellowship which his wife established in his name is a relatively enduring memorial, though with a fluctuating monetary value. But the historic import of his life and work is an entirely different matter.

His professional distinction lies in epistemology and the philosophy of religion. The Problem of Knowledge, published in 1915, was labelled by four writers of the Festschrift that honored him, as a "monumental study" and, indeed, a "classic," while his monistic critical realism was an achievement no one had matched prior to his death. R.W. Sellars was ten years later than that in adding significant scientific refinements and twenty eight years after Macintosh had elaborated his findings most fully. His historic epistemological status seems, therefore, established.

The import of these findings for both philosophy and religion must not, moreover, be underestimated. They added an intellectually assured external dimension to people's universe. I can, I think, best suggest the expansion this entailed by examples of two large mirrors I have had. Each expanded the room it was in, the first to include a segment of the Susquehanna River and of the bridge that crossed into Lewisburg, Pennsylvania; the much larger second one did not yield the same type of dramatic vista but did open the already substantial room to encompass the sparkling of aspen, birch and other trees in its purview.

Monistic critical realism offered immeasurably more, moreover, than the mirroring of areas of an external world. Macintosh thought of perceptual knowing in terms of a searchlight that directly illumined a firm external cosmos and showed its extension to the galaxies of stars.

The monistic realist, as I have evidenced in this essay, also finds that there is an important place for ideals in this universe, but, as a <u>critical</u> realist, he acknowledges that the universe is far from a philosophical idealist's dream. It is one of great wonders, indeed, yet also of earthquakes, volcanoes, hurricanes, floods, and conniving, torturing brutes. It is a universe in constant process that can only locally, partially, and temporarily be stopped. Macintosh, as Randolph Miller mentions, is quite hopitable to process philosophy.[1]

Religiously, this wondrous, yet often harsh, ongoing universe is not presented to "scare the hell out of," or into people, but as one that, first of all, bespeaks the constancy of God and yet also requires and bestirs strong moral fiber while offering opportunity for varyingly significant services and accomplishments. That there is likewise opportunity for exploiters is part of the factual yet likewise moral picture. Courageously honest people are challenged to cope with and disarm exploiting individuals and systems. This is not a world for simple passive piety, though that may be one kind of ideal, or, at least, a motivating dream.

This, of course, leads us to theology and the philosophy of religion: the former centering in the doctrine about God and his relations with the personal and impersonal world; the latter in the meaning and import of religion on the basis of all of its relevant data, and more profoundly, in the examination of the assumptions and implications of theologies as such. In Macintosh's own philosophy of religion he found himself much concerned with the religious values of the diverse philosophies, in his effort to determine which offered the best basis for the *best* religion. The philosophical basis of religion was for him a theological fundamental. But this was not original with him. G.B. Foster and the Chicago Pragmatists had been using the conception as had other philosophers and theologians, ancient, medieval, and modern. But it was Macintosh who starting from common sense realism, exploring scepticism and agnosticism, along with idealism, imbued himself with Chicago pragmatism, and went on to find a realism which could meet the needs of the most adequate religion. It was he who, as of his era, systematically advanced the conception of vital religion at its best by exploring the alternatives in contemporary philosophical realisms and examining the religious values in all distinct philosophies, including, as they came on the scene, both existentialism and phenomenology. He found the most adequate philosophy in the monistic critical realism he personally developed. While having kinship enough on this realistic basis, with the diverse views to utilize all evidential data, his basic concern was with the certifications of science and a direct surmounting of the subjectivisms of the historic empiricisms. He developed his basic religious thinking in five volumes: <u>Theology as an Empirical Science</u> (1919), <u>The Reasonableness of Christianity</u> (1925), <u>The Pilgrimage of Faith in the World of Modern Thought</u> (1931), <u>Religious Realism</u> (1931), and <u>The Problem of Religious Knowledge</u> (1940). The last three are each more inclusive and representative.

In the <u>American Spirit of Theology</u> (1974), Randolph Miller treats Mac's contribution to empirical theology.[2] He distinguished two historical stages prior to that of Macintosh. The first was that of its beginnings with Friederic Schleiermacher and Rudolf Otto. Finding the essence of religion to consist in the feeling of absolute dependence, Schleiremacher became known as the founder of modern theology. Otto added the conception of the <u>numinous</u> or holy to the demarking of religion. He found it to be a non-moral category in its initial understanding: a sensing of a <u>mysterium tremendums</u> or overwhelming mystery, combining a feeling of utter deference and compelling awe. There was no methodology involved in this first stage.

A second stage began when Lewis F. Stearns in 1890 undertook to develop <u>The Evidences of Christian Experience</u>, and William Newton Clarke followed with a kindred procedure. But for both men the experiences were subjective. The Chicago School soon began, however, to move toward objectivity with historical and sociological studies of religion.

The third stage was that of direct attempts at objectivity, first with sense data and then with the experience of relationships. For Macintosh, the approach was two-fold: 1) with a diagnosis of sensory perception; and 2) with a demarking of an experimental science of religion. The complexity of the perceptual process is pointed out, together with the directness of its perceptual references. We shall have occasion later to note the comparable complexities in three proposed philosophical alternatives--existential, Whiteheadean, and, more especially, phenomenological perceptions--with their somewhat less directness of objective observations. That they add significant data that supports Mac's "perception-in-a-complex" shows its enduring merit. The process factor in the complex could still be more clearly distinguished than it is in either Mac's realism or phenomenological analysis.

Its applicability to our experiences of God is even less clear. I shall deal with that after I have presented the three proposed alernatives to Mac's empiricism in theology. The experimental component of his empiricism will, of course, also be on trial with his evidences for the "right religious adjustment" and its disclosures.

The proposed alternatives are all presented in a single publication on The Future of Empirical Theology (Bernard E. Meland, editor,[3] University of Chicago Press, 1969). The occasion is the Centennial of the University of Chicago Divinity School. Bernard E. Meland gives both the introductory 62-page essay and another on the question, "Can Empiricism learn something from Phenomenology?" I shall present his relevant data, along with those of Schubert M. Ogden[4] in the first official essay, on "The Present Prospects of Empirical Theology" and of Daniel Day Williams[5] on "Suffering and Being in Empirical Theology." I shall cite a couple of the other eleven contributors from a scatter of theological institutions for incidental additions. The three I present will all view Macintosh as, in varying degrees, passe. It will, I hope, be illuminating to note the extent to which this is not so.

Although Meland writes on behalf of the whole group and has his own significantly constructive theological viewpoint, I shall start with Ogden's distinction of three diverse types of empiricism: sensory, existentialist and Whiteheadean non-sensory perception. Linguistic empiricisms get references in the volume, while the diverse modes of sensory empiricism are limited to its classical, instrumentalist, and "radical" varieties. The whole realistic development is omitted. We shall also by-pass it for the present, along with the classical version of Empiricism which I have presented rather fully in Chapter II.

How now does the existential view of experience differ from that of the sensory empiricists? Existentialists, Ogden explains, have been concerned with experience in a broader, deeper, richer, and more immediate sense than that of the sensory empiricists. This most immediate awareness is, indeed, the very heart of "lived experience," disclosing to human individuals their bodies (and selves) in contrast with, yet relationship to, other beings. Some existentialists have thought of man in hyphenated fashion as being-in-the-world, rather than as a perceiving subject who sees reality as assorted objects in external locations.[6] The emphasis on the relatedness of man in-and-with nature, has led to a special stress on emotive subjectivities. Fear, anxiety, anguish, dread and the whole range of inner turmoils that seem to have been given quite free reign by some existentialists. Emphasis on subjectivities is liable to this hazard, and external circumstances that leave one's life in chaos as in the defeat of everything one has believed in--by war with its direct brutalities or by other developments--may induce such subjectivities. That depth experiences must, indeed, be given full recognition in an adequate philosophy is quite generally recognized. But it must surely be kept in perspective and here the need for a more objective outlook comes to the fore.

Does Ogden's third type of empiricism provide this? Whitehead undertook to "offer a clear alternative to the 'sensationalist doctrine' which," he stated, "has been paramount in modern philosophy since Descartes."[7] Whitehead sought to do this through a doctrine of non-sensuous perception which he believed to be more rudimentary than sensuous perception. That some of its varieties are not as non-sensory as he seemed to think (bodily awareness is an instance) does not affect his contention, since he is evidently taking specialized types of sense perception as the prototype. For Whitehead, in consequence, the basic mode of experience is not "presentational immediacy" but an "intuitive awareness of our own past mental and bodily states and of the wider world beyond as they compel conformation to themselves in the present,"[8] hence, he offered a type of what

Macintosh called "perception-in-a-complex" which he considered one of four types of intuition,[9] but which, according to Whitehead, is entirely drawn from non-sensuous perception." For him, in consequence, the whole notion of our massive experience of the self, the world and others "conceived as a reaction to clearly envisaged data, is fallacious . . . the details are a reaction to the totality."[10] Gestalt psychology would probably support Whitehead in this, as would studies in child psychology from the first building of the experience of identifying the mother, and, considerably later, the father, and then other persons and things, yet the importance of developing clear perceptions and accurate knowledge remains--in spite of Meland's reformulation of Whitehead's words to "seek simplicity and distrust it" to "seek clarity and distrust it."[11] (Macintosh himself considered doubt a component of faith and faith as a state needing to be grounded on the maximum of certifiable knowledge.) Hence, Whitehead worked at formulating what he conceived as a system of accurate conceptions.[12]

How now does this Whiteheadean empiricism relate to theology? From his procedure in disentangling the details from the experience of the Whole (or Totality), Whitehead went on to the emergence of the sense of value or Importance. Discriminations of things "that matter" to the self, or to his or her interests, bring out gradations of value and the sense of the holy or what, in Rudolf Otto's terms, is to be treated with utter deference. And since man is a component of a whole related to and dependent on an over-arching providence, the holy relates most especially to God who, because of our lives intertwine with his, must have a Consequent Nature as well as a Primordial one. The sense of <u>historic</u> Importance, in turn, is an "intuition of the universe as everlasting process unfailing in its deistic unity of ideals."[13] We shall not explore God's Consequent and Primordial natures except to say that Ogden does not argue against the objection that experience does not justify so comprehensive an empiricism, yet he is convinced that the type of empiricism Whitehead elaborated is sufficiently close to our experience that no one can honestly dismiss it. The "directed activities of mankind," to which Whitehead asks attention, surely give point to a conception of nature to which our more universal intuitions are native. Still, Ogden concludes, "This expression of conviction" is simply intended to show why "I myself incline to be hopeful about the future of empirical theology."[14]

Does Meland, now, get beyond Whitehead's empiricism and process philosophy to which he had been introduced by Wieman? Meland's treatment of Macintosh was certainly cavalier. It is not to prejudice the reader that I quote it here in full:

> "A variation upon both the appeal to religious experience in the evangelical liberal sense and the empiricism of the Chicago school, and in a sense a mediation between them, is to be found in the theology of Douglas Clyde Macintosh. Macintosh was a graduate of the Divinity School of the University of Chicago. When the dean of the Yale Divinity School was considering inviting Macintosh to join their faculty, he wrote [Dean Shailer] Mathews asking about Macintosh as a theologian and scholar. Mathews spoke highly of Macintosh's gifts as a theological thinker, and ended by saying, 'If you don't hire him, we probably will.' Had Macintosh

> come to Chicago, he would have introduced
> into the Chicago scene a kind of empirical
> study of religion that would have added a
> note of dissonance to Chicago theology. For
> his concern at that time was not with reli-
> gion as a social process, but with religious
> experience as it appeared in the ordinary
> person or church member. His hope was to
> create a clinical theology that could be
> explicit in guiding the work of the minister
> among his parishioners as medical science has
> been able to inform and discipline the work
> of physicians in their communities. Theology
> as an empirical science, therefore, which was
> the title of one of his early books, was to
> consist in discovering and formulating the
> basic laws underlying the religious response,
> together with the principles of behavior ap-
> plicable to religious experience. In this
> theology, intutition, observation and reflec-
> tion were to be given parallel if not equal
> weight and emphasis."[15]

It is interesting that Meland does not treat the later divergences that came to Chicago Divinity School as other than challenges. Perhaps it was because Ogden had already written somewhat more complete statements of the Wieman-Macintosh debate that he felt justified in giving Macintosh an incomplete and rather one-sided treatment. Yet, he also totally leaves out all actual "realisms."

Ogden, I have said, gives a fairer account of the Macintosh-Wieman debate (in the <u>Christian Century</u>, in 1932), on the question "Is there a God?" Both theologians, he said, "were committed to the proposition that theology should be genuinely empirical," but, from Macintosh's standpoint, Wieman's "doctrine of a Superhuman God without a Superhuman Soul or Mind, or Conscious Intelligence and Will was strongly reminiscent of behaviorism in psychology. It succeeded in adding to the assurance <u>that God is</u> only by subtracting so drastically and, it would seem permanently, from <u>what God means</u>. If, indeed, it should turn out that the idea of God as a Superhuman Mind and Will cannot be believed in, even Wieman's ingenious, interest in and valuable definitions will hardly save the day for much that has been most dynamic and uplifting in the best religion." For Wieman, contrarily, Macintosh's attempts to show the truth of the scriptural idea of God required him to sacrifice the certainty which only a strict empiricism can provide. Macintosh, Wieman claimed, develops a system of concepts about which God ought to be instead of applying observation and reason to the actual God he has. "The religion of infallible devotion must take the place of the religion of infallible belief" [which Mac never claimed]. "We must have certainty [about the reality of God] at least as great as we have for the existence of wife or child or home. . . . When preservation of the content [of faith] is reversely proportional to the preservation of certainty, then the content must go."[16] But for Macintosh who believed in the possibility of empirical certitude about God, the God we need for life at its best is the one to be empirically certified. He could accept nothing less. And this he believed is what the historic religious tradition pointed to. Between Wieman and Macintosh there was, in consequence, an impasse which Ogden said has likewise attended "current attempts at empirical theology." His presentation of Whiteheadean empiricism, he thinks, is pointing in the right direction. What now can we say for Meland's findings regarding post Wieman-Macintosh theology?

He finds a converging of phenomenology and empiricism following the side-tracking of the latter by instrumentalism. Wieman, Whitehead, and Charles Hartshorne had gotten it back on, and carried it forward from, the track of the radical empiricism of James. Phenomenology, likewise, had gone through a change from its logical studies to inquiries in the perceptual field, thereby disclosing the depth and richness of "lived experience." Combining phenomenology with existentialism, Merleau Ponty, indeed, finds the self and the world as a configuration that bespeaks or constitutes a unity. And while subjectivity is still of prime importance, it is never viewed as "a closed track of internal thinking." There is intentionality about it [as some of the American critical realists already have shown without due accrediting]. For Ponty, this intentionality is "a dynamic structure of experience" that integrates the individual mind with the full cultural world of meaning and valuation, and brings one's funded social inheritance to bear on his present thought and activity. Meland sees in this nature of experience a recognition of both Whitehead's prehensions and his causal efficacies. I see in it a significant filling out of Machintosh's "perception-in-a-complex," expressive of the apperceptive nature of insight and intuition. We have a rather clear statement by Meland, indeed, on page 297, of <u>The Future of Empirical Theology</u>, of an apperceptive phenomological component. After stating that our "conceptualization provided us with but a 'margin of intelligibility,'" he wrote, "To these rather formal designs of immediate experience, I introduced the notion of the <u>structure</u> of experience which carried more concrete meaning, implying distillations of past events as they persisted within the cultural orbit of meaning of a people. . . ."

Parenthetically, Whitehead's use of the term "intuition," which is a similar idea, is more than paralleled by Mac's distinction of four types of intuition: rational, appreciative, imaginal, and perceptual; the first two concerning "axiomatic" truth and intrinsic value; the latter pair with certainty of reality as present and certitude of truth about reality that is not presented. Perceptual intuition may, in fact, be quite complex, involving a diversity of mental processes that include memory and imagination as well as sensing and reasoning, and so with much from personal and social history, and referring to specific things in a complex of entities in process. Mac himself does not seem to have done justice to this objective complexity and yet I have for many years utilized that extensibility. That there is a directness to perception, regardless of the processes and mechanisms involved, is the point that Macintosh was concerned to make and which I have dealt with in Chapter V.

This directness of perception is not clear in either Ponty or Meland, or, in fact, Ogden who writes about the "objectification of reality through sense perception."[17] Meland, in turn, phrases Merleau Ponty's conception regarding the openness of subjectivity to external events that while "subjectivity is still of prime importance, it is . . . the immediate access to what opens out into the world of lived experience."[18] It does not itself have direct access to the world but to the door that "opens" into the world. Meland's empiricism, in consequence, still carries relics from classical subjective empiricism. To that extent it is indirect rather than direct, and a "margin" of conceptual intelligibility is made more intelligible.

As for the theological possibilities in his empiricism, like William James he finds a MORE in the world of experience that cannot be pinpointed as a specific this or that but remains a rather impersonal *what* that is a factor beyond our own efforts and capacities, associated with our experiences of grace and judgment, the latter disciplining us and disclosing a cosmic place for both basic and ideal values.

Donald Day Wiliams comes much closer to articulating an empirical basis for faith in a conscious living God in his examination of "Suffering and Being in Empirical Theology." He starts with a broad definition of suffering that encompasses existentialist anxieties and anguishes. To suffer is to undergo, as in labor (Latin--patior). Childbirth is evidently one model with its work as well as intensities of pain. All the things that have to be done are by no means all pleasant but often highly taxing, comprise another set of instances. Suffering in this inclusive sense can be wholly mental or any combination of what we endure both physically and mentally. The threat of non-existence ("non-being" in Hegelian thinking) is evidently rather terrifying to some.

Williams is specifically concerned, however, with the constructive aspects of suffering rather than its pathology. He distinguishes three such aspects: identification, communication and healing. In numerous ways suffering enables us to find and delineate, or define, ourselves--and others. The discovery of what we can face up to and endure are among its revelations. Suffering, similarly, brings out capacities for understanding others, for communicating with them, and sharing deeper and more meaningful experiences and values. It helps, in consequence, to mold people into a community: to preserve, protect and defend their mutually basic interests, and to collaborate for better or worse in sickness and in health. "What is at stake in the understanding of suffering," Williams writes, "is crucial for the [very] possibility of human existence. . . ."[19]

"Suffering objectified," thirdly, "can become a healing power." To obtain a factual analysis of our ills is, of course, to do away with the dread of what we do not understand and to take "steps" toward our recovery, if the ailment is not terminally lethal. Should it be the latter, we may, indeed, adjust to that circumstance with considerable clearheadedness. If otherwise than terminal, psychoanalysts have shown that the "relationship in which the feelings of one are taken into the consciousness of another without rejection, without fear, and in love, is a condition of the [healthy] transformation of the self."[20] Hence, "suffering becomes constructive . . . when it participates in structures that have elements of strength. . . . It is the strength which allows the suffering to be faced that makes its transformation possible."[21] Suffering may, therefore, have causal efficacy.

How now does such an examination of suffering contribute to our understanding of God? There are two ways, writes Williams. The first is by pointing out that what works for men and women in the creative employment of suffering is not primarily human will action and design, but the action of God. We experience the weaving together into one community of being of many strands of action, feeling, pain, language, memory and expectation. Man is in the weaving, but he is not the weaver (this is a special instance of James' and Meland's MORE). "Dr. Wieman's way of pointing to the presence of God as the creative event in experience is", states Williams, "the foundation of empirical theology." "My only footnote here," he writes, "is that one way of approaching the empirical argument for God is through an analysis of the work of suffering in the creative event."[22] Some would still maintain that this is as far as we can go empirically toward knowledge of God.

Williams holds, however, that through religious commitment, "we can develop the metaphysical doctrine of God's being in relation to all of the categories. . . . The community of being in which we participate is not the human community alone, but the community of man with nature and with God." And "what we know about suffering as identification, communication and healing can become fruitful for our doctrine of the being of God. The way is thus opened to an empirical interpretation of the confessional tradition of God's creative and redemptive action" as in Romans 5:8, and "No phenomenological analysis will exhaust the depth here revealed."[23] (We have here, in consequence, a specialized version of Macintosh's "experimental" religious adjustment).

Williams' presuppositions are that there is a community of real things with analogous structures that form a field of dynamic processes. "Structure, process and valuation are the ultimate metaphysical elements. The ground of the commonality of structures is God's metaphysical function as the form-giving and power-sustaining factor in all things. He is the indispensible participant in every world. . . . A community of beings with analogous structures is the formal mode of the participation of God in the creatures and the creatures in God."[24]

"I hold," he says, "that God does suffer as he participates in the ongoing life of the society of being." Note the singular "being" rather than beings. "His sharing in the world's suffering is the supreme instance of knowing, accepting and transforming in love the suffering which arises in the world." Because of God's suffering in his transmutation of our suffering, we are "released toward the realization of our higher hopes, through what God continually does."[25]

How much of this can be called really empirical is, indeed, a problem, though Williams has tried to give an empirical interpretation of redemptive Christianity. His advance beyond Macintosh, moreover, is not clearly discernable. They share a basic religious commitment and faith in a God of utter love, expressed most notably in Jesus as Christ. Yet, Williams does not expressly write of God in terms of consciously intelligent will. The element of personal conviction rather than empirical demonstration seems to guide his conclusion.

I shall now, in consequence, undertake to sum up for Macintosh. He was not, in fact, just an empiricist. Meland's statement that Mac's theology, "intuition, observation and reflection were" to be "given parallel, if not equal, weight and emphasis" is part of thee methodological procedure we find in empirical science. The initial intuition is, as I have shown, the perception itself or, rather, the perceptions themselves, from which empirical inquiry starts. And empirical science which yields our most assured empirical knowledge is far more than empirical observations. It involves the recognition of a question to be answered or problem to be solved and, in Dewey's phrasing, a clarification of the nature of the problem sufficiently to enable the investigator to formulate hypotheses that do not fit the evidences, or to reformulate those that seem to hold promise; to repeat the tests and under a sufficiently diverse set of conditions so that one has the assurance of an adequate set of samples, and then to generalize as far as the data permit. Perceptual intuition, which we have also found in Whitehead, the existentialists, and phenomenologists is involved, along with observation and reflection, and while Mac's scientific empiricism was not identical with Dewey's, the components were quite similar. The conceptual and inferential elements are involved with the perception.

It must be recalled, indeed, that Mac was steeped in Pragmatism when he came to Yale and that he retained significant residues of it both in, and with, his monistic critical realism. Macintosh, as we noted at the end of Chapter VI, distinguished two other components of theology besides it empirical grounding. There is, he emphasized, a normative outreach and character, a stress on values and, indeed, perfections. And for him, thirdly, there is the metaphysical actuality of the divine object. Hence we have empirical, normative and metaphysical constituents of an adequate theology.

Macintosh, moreover, was a philosopher of religions as well as a theologian. Religious focus on God, while indispensable, is only one of its essentials. Its concern for values per se is another essence--as Macintosh's Chicago studies disclosed; likewise its consciousness of the need and basic importance of knowledge, and of the special values religious insight. Then there are the personal and social outreaches of religion, together with its organization and polity, and of course its conceptualization. It is a many facetted thing, with depth and height and breadth. It does not merely offer a narrow path, though it does point to a discerning one. The place for overbeliefs in religion which Macintosh distinctively recognized, along with its experimentalism, disclosed the religious role of higher vistas along with moral cautions, in the need of an adequately intelligent, working faith.

I wish now to point out and emphasize the openended nature of Macintosh's philosophy of religion. It began with his own concern for what the existentialists and phenomenologist have labelled "lived experience." Concrete experiences and immediacies were not just their concern, but their approaches to them were generally with the special and more intense types of experience, whereas Macintosh started with the experience of the common man, Mr., Miss and Mrs. average citizen. He was concerned to articulate for them, and to clarify and shape up the vaguer recognitions that function in daily life. He was concerned also, of course, with the gamut or range of human experiences, for the intensely problematic issues that people face, as in the case of G.B. Foster and the even more emotive cases of depth psychology. Existentialist concerns seem to have been a more specialized, collatoral development.

It must be recognized, moreover, as Joseph Haroutunian has pointed out in his contribution to this symposium,[27] that there is a large gap between the religious thinking of Mr. and Mrs. parishioner and the theologians, so that what Macintosh said about the liabilities of Wieman's completely empirical God are a general indication of the breadth of the gap and the loss of religious meaning involved, as in such language as Paul Tillich's when he talks of "God beyond God." Mr. parishioner, however, does live in a world of science and technology, so that what Bertrand M. Loomer presents from that standpoint would come closer to making sense. I suspect, in fact, that while Loomer's complete following of Whitehead might have raised some Macintosh queries, Meland's statement of what Loomer found in Whitehead shows a startling similarity to what Macintosh himself had been doing. Note, these quotations that could have also been said of Mac. "The theologian never escapes some philosophical orientation." "The systematic expression of Christian orientation calls for the most rigorous and thorough-going restatement of the logic of Christian faith. . . . For this purpose it behooves one," he insists, "to avail oneself of that philosophy that provides the most adequate resources for such a task." "Philosophy, for Loomer, becomes a kind of vision of the mind within with certain reflection can be carried on in a disciplined and responsible way." "This procedure," as Loomer pursues it, "becomes a subtle act of interrelating the claims of faith and reason, and of achieving through this interrelationship a constructive statement of faith that is answerable to modern intelligence, even as it presumes to be coherent with what has been historically sustained within the community of faith."[28] Mac would, I am sure, insert the words "achieved and" before "sustained" in the last sentence. But Loomer would probably do so also.

It was Macintosh's conception of the experimental nature of religion that enabled him to think in terms of its historic progress. Its advancement is evident in such biblical books as the Psalms, Isaiah, Hosea, the Gospels, and Pauline writings. There have been both recessions and advances in religion. It has had periods in which the warring spirit took over and religious people dispatched their enemies, often with great piety. "Better a wilderness than a land of heretics,"[29] was a representative view. But the purifiers of religion and refiners of its conceptions have repeatedly come to the fore, eliminating its more primitive and less high-minded components and stresses and advancing to clearer conceptions and purer values. The present struggles in empirical science and hospitality to data are both essential to its further advance, and Macintosh bespoke both.

This seems a good point at which to inject the question Wieman posed of Macintosh's ground of certainty about his conscious God of highest values (or perfections). His thesis is that the God man needs exists, and man needs a God of perfect moral and other values. From a scientific standpoint, that is an hypothesis. No scientific experiment has been able to establish that fact and empirical observation of God is not susceptible of the same sort of public feedback we get in mundane perceptions. Here, if anywhere, is where phenomenologists might have something to offer as students of phenomena, but they do not seem to have gone beyond Macintosh who made an intensive study of mystic's claims of experience. The result was that he thought the mystics might be right in their affirmation of experiencing a divine One, though they were clearly wrong in their denials of evil and a material world. And their affirmations about God, apart form an awareness of something marvellous, were stateable only in such negatives as "incomprehensable." They were, in other words, still mystified.

A better case seems makeable for such discerningly intelligent, religious persons as Admiral Richard Byrd and the astronauts who walked on the moon. Byrd spent winters in the area of the South Pole, and wrote about his sensing there the presence of God. Similarly the astronauts in the desolateness of the moon. These could be legitimate cases of "perception-in-a-complex," or they could simply be resurgences of the pieties in which they had been imbued. How do we determine which or what? After many years, I can now understand W.E. Hocking's claim to a perception of other mind in his observations of an external universe. But I still do not find any real justification for such a claim other than the evidence that we humans share a basically common world. That God may speak to us through the world's events is another matter, though Sellars wrote that he saw no evidence that the universe was "deiform." Yet, he also wrote the query, "Why is there anything rather than nothing," and that one could have a sense of wonder and awe in this world of great emergents. Are events of the world the hinderparts of God, as my Acadia Professor, H.T. DeWolfe, seemed to think when he quoted God's response to Moses in Exodus 33:22-23? Is there any frontal view of God? DeWolfe thought that Jesus was the face of God. That may be a truly discerning statement. We seem at times to recognize God in and through great personages, along with our awareness that there is creativity, and it is something we ourselves have to acknowledge in our on-going world. That there is also great love and great mindedness in this earthy sphere, that our own lives are recipients of "grace," as well as of misfortunes, the latter of which is often the fault of people, is evidence of providence. That we can, in consequence, get a composite view of God that may well be reinforced and enriched by our adjustments to God and relationships with Him. Living at its best has been found to include it, and religious adjustments have been found to yield their own, if private, certifications. Learned people have shown some convergence of thought about this. There is, accordingly, a clear place for intelligent faith, with our scientific empiricism providing the groundwork or foundation.

Joseph E. Boodin's "Spirit of the Cosmos" is a good example of a scientifically oriented philosopher who did see the universe as deiform, and, as I mentioned in Chapter VI, Macintosh published Boodin's "God and the Cosmos" in the symposium on <u>Religious Realism</u>. The ongoing processes of the universe as it functions in fields, he finds to be strong evidence for the God of our now discerning community of faith.

Two strictures must, however, be entered here that effect the limits Mac would place on the hospitality or openness of his format or system. They concern the conceptions of process philosophy and organicism respectively. The conceiving of structure and process without their focus in individual entities or beings is like Alice's thinking of a smile without a smiler. Some of the writers of this symposium seem at times to treat individuals in such incidental fashion as to regard <u>structure and process</u> as the realities. But structure and process of what? Religiously this is of paramount importance, and philosophically also.

That Mac had a clear place for process in his philosophy was shown most evidently in his use of Bergson's conception of continuous change in his class discussion of freedom of choice. Bergson's idea, he said, could be applied to human character and conduct. One might, indeed, give more or less attention to alternative courses of action, thereby delaying one's action and giving oneself opportunity to explore the consequences of each course of action and the ways by which it may be most satisfactoy. That conduct, in turn, will leave its deposit on character and facilitate or militate against further reflectively directed action. Macintosh, indeed, quoted Whitehead on relevant occasions, and, yet, held that the disposition to eliminate substantial entities entirely must be put back in balance.

The recognition of organisms as the basic type of reality should be a recognition of entities or substances per se, but some treatments focus on organic structure and process to the neglect of the substantial element in individuality that is the very heart of religion. Organicists, existentialists, and phenomenologists all tend to use the term "being," with undue frequency, in the singular. But we all start our thinking from "beings."

Historically also, organicisms have suppressed the individuality from which they started. Hegelian philosophy is the examplar. Having, in consultation with Macintosh, written my doctoral thesis on <u>Pantheism in Neo-Hegelian Thought</u>, I am particularly aware of organicism's liability to the submergence of, or loppings off, of individuals in an all-inclusive Absolute, and the denials of ignorance, error, and evil that are at least implicit.

Macintosh, of course, recognized the interrelationships and interdependence of individuals on all levels of existence and the extensibility of the term organic to things beyond the self. But to treat entities at all levels as organisms, and all of them together as an organism, is to take a rather clear biological term and apply it beyond the point where important distinctions should obtain. Macintosh insisted on this, and that the great message of the higher religions is one which while it stresses love of others and mutual aid to each other does so with concern for persons as developing individualities. The concept of organism is a focal one, but not in sweeping sense in which its basic meaning is not only diluted but even destroyed. Donald Day Williams's use of the term "community" with its many inter-relations is, indeed, a welcome change to the overworked terms "organism" and "organicism." The existential and phenomenological emphasis on concrete, lived experience accords, of course, with this contention.

Macintosh's monistic critical realism is, I have endeavored to point out, a format which not only provides hospitably for all relevant data, and undertakes to do so perspectively, on proper balance, yet also undertakes to be more than a format or system. I have dealt with his monistic realism in Chapters V and VI, showing its distincion from the new or neo-realisms and other critical realisms, as well as from common sense realism, and the variously less realistic empiricisms. A direct, discriminating perception of realities is its keynote. Yet, he conceived it as a whole, living philosopy. The extent to which he succeeded in this is suggested by the following evidences. In his theological autobiography in 1932 he relates that, in 1907-1909, while working on his doctoral thesis, he was teaching at Brandon College, Brandon, Manitoba, following his presentation of a critical paper on "The New Theology" (of R.J. Campbell) which after three years at the University of Chicago he found sadly inadequate as an interpretation of Christianity--though it would have been acceptable in his years at McMaster. The conversation

of the McMaster University made him a liberal, while amid the
"exhilerating freedom of thought and discussion" at the
University of Chicago, he soon found that he was concerned with
"conserving the vital values of Christianity." The Baptists of
Western Canada, in any case, were convinced that he had the "root
of the matter" in him.[30] He had, in fact, already begun his
career "toward an untraditional orthodoxy." That he could both
reach the Canadian Baptist parishoners and have the impact on his
students represented in my second Preface and the <u>Festschrift</u> in
his honor suggests something of the levels of understanding for
which his thought carried conviction.

    I shall simply say, therefore, in conclusion, that he was
a significant contributor to the stream of empirical philosophy
stemming from Aristotle via Roger and Francis Bacon to the
present empiricists in philosophy and theology, that monistic
critical realism is an important corrective of less balanced and
too often vague views, that its openness to fresh data, insights,
and vistas, shows its capacity to grow with further inquiry from
whatever angle. Although he had filled in the essentials of his
philosophical position by 1931, he was, nonetheless, still
enlarging and enriching it at the time of his stroke in 1942.

    Theologically, he was aligned with the great reformers,
and most notably with such men as John Huss and Johann Amos
Comenius. Rector (or President) of the New University of Prague,
and influenced by the personal type of religion proclaimed by the
Briton Wycliffe, Huss refused to recant when commanded to do so
<u>unless</u> he could be shown that anything which he said was wrong.

Told that it was not the church's business to show him how he was wrong, he went to the stake in 1415 for the right to have a meaningful personal religion, with intelligible beliefs.

Two centuries later the Hussite Bishop Comenius, author of a Pansophia and inheritor of the insistent attruism of Chelvicky as well as founder of modern education, "gave full content to the Reformation," according to the Czech philosopher President Thomas G. Masaryk.[31] Whether his religion held revivals comparable to some of the Baptist meetings in Mac's early life, it was the personal religion of the Czech Brethren. And the quite reflective Macintosh was a superlative instance of the combination of evangelical religion with deep learning and intensive thought.

"There were giants in those days."

APPENDIX

ANALYTICAL TABLE OF CONTENTS

OF

THE PROBLEM OF RELIGIOUS KNOWLEDGE

I. INTRODUCTORY: PRINCIPLES OF KNOWLEDGE IN GENERAL (1-12).
Knowledge and truth (1-2). Theories of knowledge (2-4). Critical monism, a form of realism (5-6). Modes of thought (6-7). Knowledge of minds (7-8). Values (8-9). General idea of the philosophy of religious knowledge (9-11). Division of the subject (11-12).

PART I: EXTREME MONISTIC REALISM IN RELIGION (13-14)

II. THE MYSTICAL THEORY OF RELIGIOUS KNOWLEDGE (15-28).
Naive realism in religion (15). Typical expressions of mystical experience and doctrine; viewsof Plotinus, Eckhart, Ruysbroeck, Tauler, Boehme, St. Catherine of Genoa, St. Catherine of Siena, Angela of Foligno, St. Teresa, St. John of the Cross, Madame Guyon, Ramakrishna, et. al. (16-36): (a) Immediate inner experience of divine reality (16-17). (b) Religious illumination and certitude of God (17). (c) Ineffableness of the religious experience and the nature of god (18-21). (d) Revelation of the unreality of matter, space and time (21-23). (e) Absorption of the self in God; revelation of the sole reality of God and of the unreality of the finite self (23-26). (f) Revelation of the unreality of evil (26-28).

III. CRITICAL EVALUATION OF RELIGIOUS MYSTICISM (29-44)
The quietistic tendency (29-31). Mystical certitude (31). The ratonalization of mysticism (31-33). Mystical intuition (33). Hallucinatory elements (33-34, 35-36). Mysticism and autohypnosis (35-37). Is mystical certitude knowledge or faith? (37-39). Mysticism and pathology (39-41). Mysticism and the subconscious (41-42). The practical value of mysticism (42-43). the good and the bad essence of religious mysticism (43-44).

PART II: MONISTIC IDEALISM IN RELIGION (45-160)

IX-IV. PSYCHOLOGICAL IDEALISM IN RELIGION (47-146).

IV. RELIGIOUS PSYCHOLOGISM (47-59).
Idealism in religion versus "religious versus "religious idealism" (47). Views of L. Feuerbach (48-50), F.A. Lange (50), J.H. Leuba (50-51), E. LeRoy (51-53), H. Vaihinger (53-54), E. Durkheim (54-56), J.M.E. McTaggart (57-59), J.M. Murry (59).

V. PSYCHIATRIC INTERPRETATIONS OF RELIGION (60-78).
Views of S. Freud (60-66), A. Adler (66-68), C.G. Jung (68-73), E.D. Martin (73-75), W. Trotter (75-77), A.G. Tansley (77-78).

VI. PHILOSOPHICAL ANTECEDENTS OF HUMANISM (79-96).
Views of John Dewey (79-96)

VII. THEOLOGICAL ANTECEDENTS OF HUMANISM (97-119).
Views of George B. Foster (97-119).

VIII. HUMANISM AND NEAR-HUMANISM (120-135).
Views of Irving King (120-121), E.S. Ames (121-125), J.R Geiger (125-126), H.C. Ackerman (126), G.B. Smith (127), A.E. Haydon (127-131), R.W. Sellars (131-133), T.V. Smith (133-134), H.W. Schneider (134), M.C. Otto (134-135).

IX. HUMANISM, ECCLESIASTICAL AND OTHER (136-146).
Views of W. Montgomery Brown (136-139), J.H. Dietrich, C.W. Reese, and C.F. Potter 139-142), W. Lippman (142-144), J.W. Krutch (144-146), G.J. Nathan (146).

X. LOGICAL AND LOGICAL-PSYCHOLOGICAL IDEALISM IN RELIGION (147-160).
1) Logical Idealism in Religion (147-156).
Views of G. Simmel (147-148), P. Natorp (148-149), W. Windelband (149), H. Munsteberg (149-150), G. Santayana (151, A.C. McGiffert (151-152), Bertrand Russell (152-154), W.R. Inge (154-155), Kirsopp Lake (155-156).
2) Logical-Psychological Idealism in Religion)156-160).
Views of B. Croce (156-159), G. Gentile (159-160).

PART III: CRITICAL MONISTIC REALISM IN RELIGION
(161-213; 357-382)

XI. RELIGIOUS PERCEPTION (163-187).
Appreciation of divine values and a divine factor in reality (163-165). Views of G.B. Smith (165), H.N. Wieman (164-171). the divine as conditioned by the right religious adjustment (170-173). cumulative definition of God (173). Religious realism (173-178). Critical monism in religion (1780187). Views of Rufus M. Jones (178), W.E. Hocking (179), Baron von Hugel (179), H. Bergson (180-181), N. Kemp Smith (181), J. Baillie (181-183), J. Oman (183-185), F.E. England (185), E.W. Lyman (185-187). Verification in religion (187).

XII. EMPIRICAL THEOLOGY (188-213).
The project of a scientific theology (188). Views of G.B. Smith (188-189). Historiometry (189-190). "Theology as an Empirical Science" (190-193). Discussion of criticisms by Pratt, Knudson, G.B. Smith, Fenn, Schaub, Coe, W.K. Wright, W.M. Horton, Galloway, Scullard, and Wobbermin (193-202), The laws of empirical theology (202-209): volitional (203-204), emotional (205-206), intellectual (206-207), and of physical and social well-being (208-209). Empirical

knowledge of divinely functioning reality (209-210).
Discussion of views of J.L. Stocks, J.W. Harvey and
John Laird (210-213).

XX. NORMATIVE THEOLOGY (357-369).
The need of supplementing empirical theology (357-358). Experienced divine value as norm for religious intuition and faith (358-360). The resultant doctrine of God (360-361). Growth of religious intuition and faith (361-362). Religious symbolism (362-363). Normative theology both valuational and existential (363-364). Religious pragmatism and the will to believe (364-365). The Christocentric norm (365-368). God's power and knowledge in religious intuition, in faith, and in normative theology (368-369).

XII. METAPHYSICAL THEOLOGY (370-382).
W.P. Montague and Wm. Adams Brown on the ways of knowing (370-371). Discussion in relation to revelation (371-373). Tentativeness and religious thought (373-374). Definition and methodology of metaphysics (374-375). Mutual relations of theology and metaphysics (374-376). Metaphysical problems (376-381). Metaphysical theology (381-382).

PART IV: DUALISTIC REALISM IN RELIGION (215-354)

XIII. ARGUMENTATIVE THEISM (217-229).
Dualism and agnosticism (217-218). Theistic argument and religious decline (218-219). St. Thomas' "five proofs" (219-220). The ontological argument (220-222). The cosmological argument (222). The anthropological argument (222). The teleological argument (222-225). Axiological arguments (225-229). Moral optimism and the reasonableness of Christianity (229).

XIV. RELIGIOUS AGNOSTICISM (230-242).
Views of Henry Mansel (230-233), Herbert Spencer et al. (233-236), and F.D.E. Schleiermacher (236-242). Schleiermacher and Kant (242).

XV. RELIGIOUS VALUE-JUDGMENTS (243-261).
Views of Albrecht Ritschl (243-250), A. Harnack (250), Otto Ritschl (250-253), Max Reischle (254-255), T. Haering (256), W. Herrmann (256-261).

XVI. EXISTENCE-JUDGMENTS BASED ON VALUE-JUDGMENTS (262-280).
Views of H. Siebeck (262-264), R.A. Lipsius (264-266), J. Kaftan (266-270), M. Schiebe (270-272), G. Wobbermin (272-280).

XVII. CRITICAL RATIONALISM (281-303).
Views of E. Troeltsch (281-295), H. Suskind (295), J. Volkelt (296-297), Rudolf Otto (297-303).

XVIII. RELIGIOUS PRAGMATISM (304-325).
Pragmatism and near-pragmatism (304-306). Varieties of religious pragmatism (306-307). Views of A.J. Balfour (307-309), Wm. James (309-314), E.H. Rowland (314-316), F.C.S. Schiller (316-317), J.E. Boodin (317-318), A.K. Rogers (318-320), E.W. Lyman (320-321), E.A. Cook (321-322), H. Bois (323-325). Representational pragmatism and moral optimism (322-323).

XIX. REACTIONARY IRRATIONALISM (326-354).
Theocentric theology, dualistic epistemology, and irrationalism (326-327). Views of S. Kierkegaard (327-333), Unamuno (333-335), Karl Barth, E. Brunner, et al. (335-348), P. Tillich (348-350), K. Heim (350), G. Aulen (350-351), A. Nygren (351), N. Berdyaev (351-354).

THE PUBLICATIONS OF

DOUGLAS CLYDE MACINTOSH

BOOKS AND PARTS OF BOOKS

The Reaction Against Metaphysics in Theology, 86 pp., Chicago:
    Published by the Author, 1911.

    Ph.D. Dissertation, University of Chicago, 1909.

The Problem of Knowledge, 503 pp., New York: Macmillan, 1915;
    London: Allen and Unwin, 1916.

God in a World at War, 60 pp., London: Allen and Unwin, 1918.

Theology as an Empirical Science, 270 pp., New York: Macmillan,
    1919, 1927; London: Allen and Unwin, 1920.

"Preface" to Christianity in its Modern Expression, by
    G.B. Foster, edited by D.C. Macintosh, New York: Macmillan,
    1921.

"Theology in a Scientific Age" in Education for Christian
    Service, by Members of the Faculty of the Divinity School
    of Yale University . . . pp. 133-162, New Haven: Yale
    University Press, 1922.

The Reasonableness of Christianity, 293 pp., New York: Scribner,
    1925, 1926; Edinburgh: Clark, 1926. Translation,
    Vernunftgemasses Christentum, mit Einfuhrung von Professor
    D.K. Bornhausen . . . Ubersetzung von O.H. Fleischer,
    166 pp. Gotha: Klotz, 1928.
    A selection from the first ten chapters was made for the
    Nathaniel W. Taylor Lectures, delivered at Yale University
    in April, 1925. The Bross Prize, 1925.

"What God Is" in <u>My Idea of God; A Symposium of Faith</u>, edited by J.F. Newton, pp. 135-158, Boston: Little, Brown, 1926. Also published as "The Meaning of God in Modern Religion," <u>Journal of Religion</u>, Vol. VI, pp. 457-471, September, 1926.

"Contemporary Humanism" in <u>Humanism, Another Battle Line</u>, edited by W.P. King, pp. 39-72, Nashville: Cokesbury, 1931.

<u>The Pilgrimage of Faith in the World of Modern Thought</u>, Stephanos Nirmalendu Ghosh Lectures, 299 pp., Calcutta, India: University of Calcutta, 1931; New York: Longmans, Green, 1931.

"Preface" and "Experimental Realism in Religion" in <u>Religious Realism</u>, edited by D.C. Macintosh, pp. v-vi, pp. 303-409, New York: Macmillan, 1931.

"Toward a New Untraditional Orthodoxy" in <u>Contemporary American Theology; Theological Autobiographies</u>, edited by Vergilius Ferm, Vol. I, pp. 275-319, New York: Round Table Press, 1932.

<u>Is There a God? A Conversation</u>, by H.N. Wieman, D.C. Macintosh, and M.C. Otto, with an Introduction by C.C. Morrison, 328 pp., Chicago: Willett, Clark, 1932. Republished with slight modifications from the <u>Christian Century</u> (Chicago), Vol. XLIX, 1932.

"Some Reflections on the Progress and Decline of Religion in New England," in <u>The Process of Religion; Essays in Honor of Dean Shailer Mathews</u>, edited by M.H. Krumbine, pp. 93-119, New York: Macmillan, 1933.

"Introduction," to <u>The Nature of Religion</u>, by G. Wobbermin, translated by T. Menzel and D.S. Robinson, New York: Crowell, 1933.

"Foreward," to <u>Polity and Practice in Baptist Churches</u>, by W.R. McNutt, Philadelphia: Judson Press, 1935.

"Romanticism or Realism, Which?" in <u>American Philsophies of Religion</u>, by H.N. Wieman and B.E. Meland, pp. 325-332, Chicago: Willett, Clark, 1936.

<u>The Plain Man's Soliloquy: A Philosophical Autobiography</u>. Microfilm, New Haven: Yale University Photographic Service, Yale University Library (MS dated 1938).

<u>The Hope of Immortality</u>, New York: Abington Press, 1938.

<u>Social Religion</u>, New York and London: C. Scribner's Sons, 1939.

<u>The Problem of Religious Knowledge</u>, New York and London: Harper Brothers, 1940.

<u>Essays in Theology and Philosophy</u>, assembled and bound by the author, 1940.

<u>Personal Religion</u>, New York: C. Scribner's Sons, 1942.

"Eternal Life," <u>Liberal Theology</u>, edited by David E. Roberts and Harry Pittney Van Dusen, New York: C. Scribner's Sons, 1942.

"Theology and Metaphysic," <u>Twentieth Century Philosophy</u>. Living Schools of Thought (Dagobert D. Runes, ed.), New York: Philosophical Library, 1943.

"The Conservation of Values," <u>Philosophies of Religion</u> (William S. Sahakian, ed.), Cambridge: Schenkman Publishing Co., 1965.

ARTICLES AND REVIEWS

"University Studies," McMaster University Monthly (Toronto), Vol. XII, pp. 153-157, pp. 153-157, pp. 210-215, January, February, 1903.

"William Rainey Harper: An Appreciation," McMaster University Monthly (Toronto), Vol. XV, pp. 241-248, March, 1906.

"The Significance of Gnosticism in the Development of Christian Theology, With Special Reference to the 'Pistis Sophis'," Review and Expositor (Louisville, Kentucky), Vol. IV, pp. 405-422, July, 1907.

"The New Theology," Review and Expositor, Vol. IV, pp. 600-617, October, 1917.

"The Function of History in Theology," American Journal of Theology, (Chicago), Vol. XI, pp. 647-652, October, 1907.

"Some Philosophical Discussions of Religious Problems," American Journal of Theology, Vol. XII, pp. 162-167, January, 1908. Review of The Freedom of Authority; Essays in Apologetics, by J.M. Sterrett, New York: Macmillan, 1905; Pragmatism: a New Name for Some Old Ways of Thinking, by William James, New York: Longmans, Green, 1907; The Religious Conception of the World: An Essay in Constructive Philosophy, by A.K. Rogers, New York: Macmillan, 1907.

"The Baptist Perspective," Western Outlook (Brandon, Manitoba), Vol. II, p. 5, March, 1909.

"Recent Expositions of the Philosophy of Religion," <u>American Journal of Theology</u>, Vol. XIII, pp. 630-633, October, 1909. Review of <u>Modern Thought and the Crisis in Belief</u>, by R.M. Wenley, New York: Macmillan, 1909; <u>The Philosophy of Revelation</u>, by H. Bavinck, New York: Longmans, Green, 1909; <u>Science and Immortality</u>, by Sir Oliver Lodge, New York: Moffat, 1908.

"Can Pragmatism Furnish a Philosophical Basis for Theology?", <u>Harvard Theological Review</u> (Cambridge), Vol. III, pp. 125-135, January, 1910. Paper read before the Baptist Congress at New York, November 9, 1909.

"Some Fundamental Problems of Modern Theology," <u>American Journal of Theology</u>, Vol. XIV, pp. 136-141, January 1910. Review of <u>Le Discernment du Miracle</u>, by P. Saintyves, Paris: Nourry, 1909; <u>Essais sur la Connaisance</u>, by G. Fonsegrive, Paris: Gabalda, 1909; <u>System Theologischer Erkenntnislehre</u>, by K. Dunkmann, Leipzig: Deichert, 1919.

"Idealism as a Practical Creed," <u>American Journal of Theology</u>, Vol. XIV, pp. 320-321, April, 1910. Review of <u>Idealism as a Practical Creed</u>, by H. Jones, New York: Macmillan, 1909.

"The Efficient Church and Current Philosophy," <u>Yale Divinity Quarterly</u>, Vol. VII, pp. 1-15, July, 1910.

"The Pragmatic Element in the Teaching of Paul," <u>American Journal of Theology</u>, Vol. XIV, pp. 361-381, July, 1910.

"Personal Idealism, Pragmatism, and the New Realism," <u>American Journal of Theology</u>, Vol. XIV, pp. 650-656, October, 1910. Review of <u>Philosophy and Religion</u>, by H. Rashdall, New York: Scribner, 1910; <u>The Principles of Pragmatism: A Philosophical Interpretation of Experience</u>, by H. Heath Bawden, Boston: Houghton, Mifflin, 1910; <u>Essays Philosophical and Psychological in Honor of William James</u>, by his Colleagues at Columbia University, New York: Longmans, Green, 1908.

"Review of <u>The Problem of Human Life as Viewed by the Great Thinkers from Plato to the Present Time</u>, by Rudolf Eucken, translated by W.S. Hough and W.R. Boyce Gibson, New York: Scribner, 1910"; <u>Yale Divinity Quarterly</u>, Vol. VII, pp. 63-64, November, 1910.

"Pragmatism and Mysticism," <u>American Journal of Theology</u>, Vol. XV, pp. 142-146, January, 1911. Review of <u>The Influence of Darwin upon Philosophy and Other Essays in Contemporary Thought</u>, by John Dewey, New York: Holt, 1910; <u>Faith and Its Psychology</u>, William R. Inge, New York: Scribner, 1910.

"Review of <u>The Meaning and Value of Human Life</u>, by R. Eucken, London: Black, 1910; <u>Christianity and the New Idealism: A Study in the Religious Philosophy of To-Day</u>, by R. Eucken, New York: Harper, 1909;" <u>Yale Divinity Quarterly</u>, Vol. VIII, pp. 16-18, May, 1911.

"The Conservative and the Radical Method in Theology and Preaching," <u>Homiletic Review</u>, Vol. LXI, pp. 359-363, May, 1911.

"Is Belief in the Historicity of Jesus Indispensable to Christian
Faith?", American Journal of Theology, Vol. XV,
pp. 362-372, July, 1911; Vol. XVI, pp. 106-110, January,
1912.

"The Idea of a Modern Orthodoxy, Harvard Theological Review,
Vol. IV, pp. 477-488, October, 1911.

"What Hinders the Union of Baptists and the Disciples of
Christ?", Proceedings, Baptist Congress, 1911, pp. 88-97,
Chicago: University of Chicago Press, 1912.

"Representational Pragmatism, Mind, N.S., Vol. XXI, pp. 167-181,
April, 1912.

"Bergson and Religion," Biblical World, N. S., Vol. XLI,
pp. 34-40, January, 1913.

"The Religion of the Future," Faith and Doubt, Vol I, pp. 94-101,
March, 1913. Republished from The Western Outlook, Vol. I,
pp. 4-5, November, 1908.

"Contemporary Philosophy and the Problem of Religion," American
Journal of Theology, Vol. XVII, pp. 307-316. April, 1913.
Review of The Positive Evolution of Religion: Its Moral
and Social Reaction, by F. Harrison, New York: Putnam,
1913; The New Realism: Co-operative Studies in Philosophy,
by E.B. Holt, W.T. Marvin, W.P. Montague, R.B. Perry,
W.B. Pitkin, and E.G. Spaulding, New York: Macmillan,
1912; The Problem of Religion, by E.C. Wilm, Boston:
Pilgrim, 1912; The Interpretation of Religious Experience,
2 v., by John Watson, Glasgow: MacLehose, 1912;

An Interpretation of Rudolf Eucken's Philosophy, by
.W.T. Jones, New York: Putnam, 1912.

"Is 'Realistic Epistemological Monism Inadmissible'?",
Journal of Philosophy, Psychology, and Scientific Method,
Vol. X, pp. 701-710, December, 1913.

"What Is the Christian Religion?", Harvard Theological Review,
Vol. VII, pp. 16-46, January, 1914.

"Hocking's Philosophy of Religion: An Empirical Development of
Absolutism," Philosophical Review, Vol. XXIII, pp. 27-47,
January, 1914.

"The Religious Philosophy of W.E. Hocking," Yale Divinity
Quarterly, Vol. X, pp. 73-80, January, 1914.
Review of The Meaning of God in Human Experience, by
W.E. Hocking, New Haven: Yale University Press, 1912.

"The New Christianity and World-Conversion," American Journal of
Theology, Vol. XVIII, pp. 337-354, pp. 553-570, July,
October, 1914.

"Haering's Dogmatics," American Journal of Theology, Vol. XIX,
pp. 304-308, April 1915.
Review of The Christian Faith: A System of Dogmatics, by
Theo. Haering, translated from the Second (1912) German
edition by John Dickie and G. Ferries, 2 v., New York:
Hodder and Stoughton, 1913.

"Professor Ten Broeke's Introduction to Theology," McMaster
University Monthly, Vol. XXIV, pp. 232-236, April 1915.
Review of Constructive Basis for Theology, by J. Ten
Broeke, New York: Macmillan, 1914.

"Christianity as Religion Made Moral," *Biblical World*, N. S.,
    Vol. XLV, pp. 195-201, April, 1915.

"A Sketch of the Philosophy of Religion, With Illustrations of
    Critical Monism," *Mind*, N. S., Vol. XXVIII, pp. 129-161,
    April, 1919.

    Substantially the same as The Appendix to *Theology As an
    Empirical Science*, 1919.

"Troeltsch's Theory of Religious Knowledge," *American Journal of
    Theology*, Vol. XXIII, pp. 274-289, July, 1919.

"Why I Believe in Immortality," *Biblical World*, N. S., Vol. LIV,
    pp. 570-573, November, 1920.

"A Neo-Realist's Conception of God," *Journal of Religion*
    (Chicago), Vol. II, pp. 92-97, January, 1922.

    Review of *Space, Time and Deity*, by S. Alexander, 2 v.,
    London: Macmillan, 1920.

"A Defense of Christian Theism," *Journal of Religion*, Vol. III,
    pp. 214-215, March 1923.

    Review of *Studies in Christian Philosophy*, by
    W.R. Matthews, London: Macmillan, 1921.

"The Idea of God," *Journal of Religion*, Vol. III, pp. 652-655,
    November, 1923.

    Review of *The Idea of God*, by C.A. Beckwith, New York:
    Macmillan, 1922.

"Books That Help Faith," *Christian Century* (Chicago), Vol. XLI,
    pp. 1370-1371, October 23, 1924.

"Religious Values and the Existence of God," *Journal of Religion*,
    Vol. VI, pp. 315-320, May 1926.

Review of <u>Religious Values</u>, by E.S. Brightman, New York: Abingdon, 1925.

"The Baptists and Church Union," <u>Crozer Quarterly</u> (Chester, PA.), Vol. III, pp. 259-278, July 1926.

Paper read before the American Theological Society (Eastern Branch) at New York, April 10, 1926.

"Review of <u>Mind and Its Place in Nature</u>, by D. Drake, New York: Macmillan, 1925," <u>Journal of Philosophy</u>, Vol. XXIV, pp. 129-136, March, 1927.

"Review of <u>A Theory of Direct Realism and the Relations of Realism to Idealism</u>, by J. E. Turner, New York: Macmillan, 1925; <u>Personality and Reality; A Proof of the Real Existence of a Supreme Self in the Unvierse</u>, by J.E. Turner, New York: Macmillan, 1926;" <u>Journal of Philosophy</u>, Vol. XXIV, pp. 157-159, March, 1927

"Professor Coe and an Empirical Theology," <u>Methodist Quarterly Review</u> (Nashville), Vol. LXXVI, pp. 202-218, April, 1927.

"Canon Streeter's Theory of Reality," <u>Journal of Religion</u>, Vol. VIII, pp. 147-151, January, 1928.

Review of <u>Reality: A New Correlation of Science and Religion</u>, by B.H. Streeter, New York: Macmillan, 1926.

"The Next Step in Epistemological Dialectic," <u>Journal of Philosophy</u>, Vol. XXVI, pp. 225-233, April 1929.

Paper read, with some omissions, before the American Philosophical Association (Eastern Division), at the University of Pennsylvania, December 28, 1928.

"Religious Knowledge and Reasonable Faith," Colgate-Rochester
　　　Divinity School Bulletin (Rochester, New York), Vol. II,
　　　pp. 160-174, November, 1929.

"Review of Individuality and Social Restraint, by G.R. Wells,
　　　New York: Appleton, 1929;" Bulletin of the Hartford
　　　Seminary Foundation (Hartford, Connecticut), Vol. XVI,
　　　pp. 122-124, May-June, 1930.

"Christianity According to Paul," Christianity Century Pulpit
　　　(Chicago), Vol. I, pp. 14-17, October, 1930.

"What Is Worship?", Religious Education (Chicago), Vol. VIII,
　　　pp. 944-946, December, 1930.

"Is Christianity Essentially Irrational?", Crozer Quarterly,
　　　Vol. VIII, pp. 16-29, January, 1931.

"Humanism Viewed and Reviewed," New Humanist, Vol. IV, pp. 16-19,
　　　July-August, 1931.

　　　Review of Humanism in Religion Examined, by Robert J.
　　　Hutcheson, Chicago: Published by the Meadville Theological
　　　School, 1931.

"Contemporary Humanism," in Humanism Another Battle Line,
　　　William P. King, ed. Nashville: Cokesbury Press, 1931.

"Disarmament," Yale Daily News (New Haven, Connecticut), Vol. LV,
　　　p. 1, November 23, 1931.

"War," Unity (Chicago), Vol. CVIII, p. 341, February, 1932.

"Conscience and War," Religion in Life (New York), Vol. I,
　　　pp. 1630168, July, 1932.

　　　Also published in The Bulletin, Crozer Theological Seminary
　　　(Chester, Pennsylvania), Vol. XXIV, pp. 133-140, July, 1932.

"What Has Professor Brightman Done to Personalism?", Religion in
Life, Vol. I, pp. 304-307, Spring, 1932.

"A Postscript to the Conversation," Christian Century, Vol. XLIX,
p. 1276, October 19, 1932.

"Mr. Wieman and Mr. Macintosh 'Converse' With Mr. Dewey,"
Christian Century, Vol. L, pp. 300-302, March 1, 1933.

"A Communication: Mr. Macintosh Restates His Position,"
Christian Century, Vol. L, pp. 531-533, April 19, 1933.

"What Is Vital in Religion?", Adult Student (Nashville,
Tennessee), Vol. XXVIII, pp. 387-388, September, 1935.

"The Hope of Immortality," Religion in Life, Vol. VII, Spring,
1938.

Two Important Books in Theology: Religion in Life, Vol. VII,
No. 3, 1939. Reviews of Hugh Ross Macintosh, Types of
Modern Theology, and John McLeod Campbell, The Legacy of
the Christian Mind.

"Empirical Theology and Some of its Misunderstanders," The Review
of Religion, May 1939.

"Theology, Valuational or Existential?", The Review of Religion,
November, 1939.

"Is Theology Reducible to Mythology?", The Review of Religion,
May, 1940.

Introduction to George Wobberman, The Nature of Religion, New
York: Crowell, 1940.

"Responsibility, Freedom, and Causality; or The Dilemma of
Determinism and Indeterminism," Journal of Philosophy,
Vol. XXXVII, November 2, January, 1940.

"The Logic of Constructive Theology," Science, Philosophy, Religion. A Symposium. Conference on Science Philosophy, and Religion, New York, 1941.

"Natural Revelation." The Dudelian Lecture for 1940-41, Harvard University, Harvard Divinity School Bulletin, Vol. XXXIX, November 14, April, 1942.

"Review of Man's Vision of God and The Logic of Theism, by Charles Hartshorne," Review of Religion, Vol. VI, November 4, 1942.

"The Method of Religious Inquiry," Religion in Life, Summer, 1945.

FOOTNOTES

PREFACE I

¹Macintosh, Douglas Clyde, "Preface" to <u>Social Religion</u>, p. x (New York and London: Charles C. Scribaer's Sons) 1939.

²<u>Social Religion</u>, pp. 285-287.

³Ibid, pp. 287-288.

⁴Ibid, p. 289.

⁵Ibid, pp. 289-292.

⁶Ibid, p. 294.

⁷Harbaugh, William H., <u>A Lawyer's Lawyer, The Life of John W. Davis</u>. (New York: Oxford University Press) 1973. p. 286.

⁸Ibid, p. 296.

⁹<u>Social Religion</u>, Preface, p. xi.

FOOTNOTES

PREFACE 2

¹Bainton, Roland H., *Yale and the Ministry* (New York: Harper and Row, 1952) pp. 227 & 232.

²Letter of '78.

³Compiled by Paul Douglas Macintosh Keane for the Macintosh Centennial. His parents were neighbors and devoted admirers of Macintosh.

⁴My account of the unveiling is based on a tape of "Reflections" supplied by Yale Divinity School Visual Education Service, together with communications from Keane and Miller.

⁵Bainton, Roland H., Brochure on the Douglas Clyde Macintosh "Fellowship in Theology and the Philosophy of Religion," p.11.

⁶Bainton, Roland H., *Yale and the Ministry*, p. 233.

⁷Brochure, pp. 1-6.

⁸Ibid.

⁹Ibid, p. 11.

FOOTNOTES

CHAPTER I

[1] Macintosh, Douglas Clyde, "Toward a New Untraditional Orthodoxy," <u>Contemporary American Theology</u>. Vol. I (Vergilius Ferm, editor), 1932, pp.282-83 (Hereinafter designattted CAT).

[2] Ibid., p. 287.

[3] This quotation and the next two are from CAT.

[4] Class notes.

[5] The examples are the writer's, not D.C.M.'s.

[6] CAT.

[7] See the Bibliography at the end of this volume.

[8] The names that occur to me most readily are Gene Adams, Eugene Bewkes, Herman Brautigam, Vergilius Ferm, Howard Jefferson, Gordon Jury, Cornelius Kruse, James Nason, F.S.C. Northrop, D.S. Robinson, George Thomas, and my own, Preston Warren. To these we can, of course, add such philosophers of Religion as J.S. Bixler, Robert Calhoun, Julian Hartt, Reinhold Niebuhr, and Richard Niebuhr to mention but five. Four of the above, Bewkes, Bixler, Jefferson, Nason, became college and university presidents.

[9] Roland Bainton, Personal letter, October 23, 1979.

[10] Letter, July 20, 1979.

FOOTNOTES

CHAPTER II

[1] The word "experience" occurs only a few times in the two testaments, depending on which version you use. My concordance lists only four instances each with a different shade of meaning, e.g. acquaintance with knowledge gained from the give-and-take of life, process of learning, and established skill. But the ideas of experience as awareness, conscious confrontation, learning activity involved in awareness, problematic, dramatic and traumatic personal ordeals--these modes of "experience," with varying insights, are common to both testaments. George E. Horr's Training of the Chosen People, which I acquired as a student in the early 1920s, featured the role of experience in the Old Testament. The training of the disciples is a cardinal feature of the New Testament, while the Pauline confrontation leading to a dramatic conversion stands out (in contrast certainly to the experiences of Mark, Luke, John, and the pastoral types in the Psalms).

[2] Augustine's religious experience was, to begin with, of Pauline type but as the Bishop of Hippo, it took on a different character.

[3] Huss, Luther, Zwingli, Calvin, and Wesley are preeminent.

[4] Douglas Clyde Macintosh, The Pilgrimage of Faith in Modern Thought (hereafter designated as PF), Calcutta: University of Calcutta Press, 1931, pp. 42-45. Cf. the parallel readings in The Problem of Knowledge (hereafter PK), New York: Macmillan

Co., 1915. Cf. also The Problem of Religious Knowledge (hereafter PRK), New York and London: Harper & Bros., 1940, pp. 13-44. Class notes (CN) are also a basic source here and throughout this biography.

[5] PK, pp. 75-79; PF, p. 210.

[6] PK, pp. 407-37; PF, pp. 155eff.

[7] On the "Pilgrimage of Faith in the World Of Modern Thought."

[8] Vergilius Ferm, Contemporary American Theology, New York: Round Table Press, Vol. II, 1932. (Herein after referred to as CAT) pp. 279-319 presents Macintosh's theological biography under the title of "Toward A New Untraditional Orthodoxy." The specific referral here is to p. 302.

[9] Available at Yale University Divinity School Library.

[10] "Pilgrimage of Faith in the World of Modern Thought" (PF), p. 41.

[11] Ibid., pp. 41-42.

[12] Ibid., pp. 44-45.

[13] Ibid., p. 46.

[14] In his Problem of Knowledge (New York: Macmillan 1915), Macintosh distinguishes two groups encompassing, at least seventeen philosophers whose agnosticism is not fully acknowledged. Cf pp. 36-71.

[15] The Problem of Knowledge (PK), p. 28.

[16] PF, p. 50.

[17] Ibid., p. 53.

[18] Ibid., p. 55.

[19] Ibid., p. 59.

[20] Ibid., p. 63.

[21] Ibid., p. 65.

[22] Ibid., p. 71.

[23] PK, p. 21.

FOOTNOTES

CHAPTER III

[1] PF, p. 75.

[2] Cf PK, pp. 93, 182, 184 and 185.

[3] PK, pp. 81-82.

[4] Ibid., pp. 84-85.

[5] Charles M. Bakewell's treatment of "the continuity of the idealist tradition" <u>Contemporary Idealism in America</u> (New York, Macmillan, 1932; Clifford Barrett, ed.) would seem to justify the claim to a great idealist tradition in philosophy, from Plato to Josiah Royce and George Holmes Howison. But Macintosh's critique of Bakewell's own idealism, presented at the end of this chapter, evidences the problem with such a contention.

[6] PK, p. 89.

[7] Ibid., p. 88. It is in the <u>Parmenides</u> that Plato discusses these problems of the Ideas.

[8] Ibid., p. 185.

[9] Ibid., p. 187.

[10] Ibid.

[11] Soliloquy, Ch. 5.

[12] This critique is based mainly on class lectures and discussions. Having written my own dissertation at Macintosh's suggestion, on <u>Pantheism in Neo-Hegelian Thought</u>, it is quite familiar ground.

[13] Class Data.

[14] Macintosh has two sections on pure mysticism in PK: pp. 75-80 and 89-91, brief treatment in PF, two chapters in PRK, with fuller expositions in his class discussion in philosophy of Religion.

[15] W.E. Hocking's is one example of a recourse to mysticism to support Absolute Idealism.

[16] PK, p. 59.

[17] Ibid., p. 58.

[18] Ibid., p. 59-60.

[19] Ibid., p. 142.

[20] Soliloquy, Ch. X, Cf notably Royce, The Problem of Christianity, (New York, Macmillan Co., 1913), Lectures IX and X, cf XI, XII, XIII and XIV.

[21] Cf Soliloquy, op. cit.

[22] PF, p. 263.

[23] Ibid., pp. 264, 265.

[24] Soliloquy, Ch. X.

[25] PK, p. 207.

[26] Ibid.

[27] Ibid, 208.

FOOTNOTES

CHAPTER IV

[1] PK, pp. 181-209.

[2] Cf. Peirce, Charles S., "Pragmatism in Retrospect," Philosophical Writings of Peirce (Justus Buchler, ed.) Routledge & Kegal Paul, 1940, p. 2 of essay.

[3] PK, p. 410.

[4] PF, p. 43.

[5] PK, p. 273.

[6] Ibid., p. 117. Experience becomes subjective when the conditions for a favorable organic response do not obtain.

[7] Ibid., pp. 225-26.

[8] Ibid., p. 227.

[9] Wright, W.K. History of Modern Philosophy, New York, Macmillan Co., 1941, p. 55.

[10] PK, pp. 418, 422-23.

[11] Ibid., p. 418.

[12] For example, As William James Said, Elizabeth Perkins Aldrich, ed., Vanguard Press, 1942.

[13] PK, p. 422.

[14] PF, p. 156.

[15] Journal of Philosophy IV, 1907, p. 313.

[16] PF, pp. 156-57.

[17] PK, p. 437.

[18] Ibid.

[19]"The Plain Man's Soliloquy," 1938, typescript microfilm, Yale Divinity School Library, Ch. XI.

[20]CAT, p. 302.

[21]PK, pp. 438-39.

[22]Ibid., pp. 439-40.

[23]Ibid., p. 440.

[24]Ibid., p. 441.

FOOTNOTES

CHAPTER V

[1] Macintosh, Douglas Clyde, *The Reasonableness of Christianity*, New York, Charles Scribner's Sons, 1931, pp. 166-67. (Hereinafter referred to as R.C.).

[2] Cf. Montague, William Pepperal, "The Story of American Realism," *Ways of Things*, New York, Prentice Hall, 1940, p. 251.

[3] R.C., p. 190.

[4] Montague, op. cit.

[5] "Program and First Platform," *Journal of Philosophy 7*, 393-401; The New Realism (E.B. Holt, ed.), New York, Macmilla, 1912.

[6] "Is Realistic Epistemological Monism Inadmissible," *Journal of Philosophy*, December 18, 1913.

[7] "Critical Realism and the Time Problem" I and II, *Journal of Philosophy, Psychology, and Scientific Methods*, 5, 542-48, 597-602; "Space," *Journal of Philosphy* . . ., 6, 617-23; "Causality," *Journal of Philosophy* . . ., 6, 323-28.

[8] The Preface to Sellars' *Critical Realism* is dated 1913. His communications with me also related that the MS was completed that year.

[9] *The Philosophy of Physical Realism*, New York, Macmillan, 1932, p. vi; "A Clarification of Critical Realism," *Philosophy of Science*, 6 (1939), 421.

[10] R.C., p. 200.

[11] Ibid.

[12] *Religious Realism*, 361-368.

[13] Ibid., 363.

[14] Ibid.

[15] *The Problem of Knowledge*, New York, Macmilla, 1915, p. 459.

[16] Ibid., pp. 491-92.

[17] Ibid., pp. 492-93.

[18] Ibid, pp. 494-95.

[19] Ibid., p. 495.

FOOTNOTES

CHAPTER VI

¹Class notes (Philosophy of Religion) (Hereinafter CN), October 12, 1926.

²*Religious Realism*, New York, Macmillan Co., 1931, p. 319 (Hereinafter RR).

³CN, see fn #1.

⁴CN (Philosophy of Religion), November 2, 1926.

⁵Quotation from my own notes. *In Religious Realism*, Macintosh's first two sentences on "Experimental Realism in Religion" are: "Religion has a double taproot. It is deeply grounded in our consciousness of reality and our seeking of values" (p. 307).

⁶*The Problem of Religious Knowledge*, Harper & Brothers, New York and London 1940, p. 97 (Hereinafter PRK).

⁷Ibid., p. 115.

⁸Ibid., pp. 114-15.

⁹Ibid., p. 115.

¹⁰Ibid.

¹¹Ibid., pp. 117-18.

¹²RR, p. 319.

¹³Ibid., p. 322.

¹⁴Ibid., pp. 322-24.

¹⁵Ibid., pp. 324-25.

[16] *The Reasonableness of Christianity*, New York, Charles Scribner's Sons 1925, pp. 239-240. (Hereinafter RC).

[17] *The Pilgrimage of Faith in the World of Modern Thought*, Calcutta, University of Calcutta Press, 1931, p. 159. (Hereinafter PF).

[18] Quoted by Macintosh in RR, p. 397.

[19] Ibid., p. 399.

[20] Ibid., p. 397.

[21] Dewey, John, *A Common Faith*, New Haven, Yale University Press: 1934, pp. 42, 51, 86.

[22] PRK, p. 95.

[23] Ibid.

[24] RR, p. 393-94.

[25] Ibid., p. 404.

[26] PRK, p. 40.

[27] CN - recollections from discussions of Mysticism in five successive class periods on Philosophy of Religion, October 19-27, 1926 and incidentally later.

[28] PRK, p. 43.

[29] Macintosh, D.C., "Theology, Valuational or Existential," *The Review of Religion*, November, 1939, pp. 36-37.

[30] Ibid., pp. 33-34.

[31] PRK, pp. 368-69.

[32] CF. "The Hope of Immortality," *Religion in Life*, Spring, 1938; "Eternal Life," *Liberal Theology, an Appraisal*, edited by David E. Roberts and Henry P. VanDusan, New York, C. Scribner's Sons, 1942, pp. 238-54.

[33]CF. "What is Vital Religion?" The Adult Student, vol. XXVIII, No. 9, September, 1935; also such statements as: "What I am interested in might more appropriately be designed modern evangelism than liberalism" (His concluding sentence in The Review of Religion, January 1940).

[34]Macintosh's review of Charles Hartshorne's Man's Vision of God and the Logic of Theism, in the Review of Religion, Vol. VI, No. 4, 1942.

FOOTNOTES

CHAPTER VII

¹Class notes (CN) in Systematic Theology, December 2, 1925.

²PRK, pp. 164-65.

³Ibid., p. 163.

⁴Macintosh, D.C., The Reasonableness of Christianity, New York, Charles Scribers Sons. 1925, ch III.

⁵PRk, p. 209.

⁶Ibid., pp. 342-43.

⁷Ibid., pp. 278-279.

⁸Ibid., pp. 284-85.

⁹Ibid., pp. 360-61.

¹⁰Religious Realism, p. 327.

¹¹Ibid., pp. 407-09.

¹²The elements of faith in Macintosh's philosophy are clearly distinguished from those of knowledge, but never in opposition to it. They are, rather, "intuitive certitudes" that supplement knowldge and provide suggestive guides toward objective certainties (PRK 373; cf 364).

FOOTNOTES

CHAPTER VIII

[1] Sent to me for comment March 5, 1968.

[2] Quoted in class.

[3] Ferm, Virgilius, Contemporary American Theology, (New York, Round Table Press), vol. I, 1931.

[4] Cf. PRK, pp. 8-9.

[5] Everett, Walter G., Moral Values, (New York, Henry Holt), 1918, p. 182.

[6] Tawney, Richard H., Religion and the Rise of Capitalism. (New York, Harcourt, Brace), 1926.

[7] Cf. Sellars, Roy Wood, "Can a Reformed Materialism do Justice to Values," Ethics, vol. 55 (1934), pp. 28-45.

[8] PRK, Preface vii.

[9] "Disarmament," Yale Daily News, New Haven, November 23, 1931.

[10] "War," Letter to the Editor of Unity, Chicago, vol. CVIII, February 1932, p. 341.

[11] Religion in Life, vol. VIII, No. 3, 1939.

[12] Social Religion (hereinafter designated S.R.), New York, C. Scriber's Sons, 1939, p. 6.

[13] Cf. References 14 and 22.

[14] SR., p. 17.

[15] Ibid.

[16] Ibid., p. 31.

[17] Ibid., pp. 34-34.

[18] Ibid.

[19] Reference to the "Second Coming" of Christ is not Macintosh's but this biographer's. I have no notations to show that he ever mentioned the second coming. It was not part of his experimental or his fundamental religion, and not in accord with what he finds to be Jesus' conception of himself.

[20] SR., p. 37.

[21] Ibid, pp. 55-56.

[22] RC, pp. 135-148.

[23] PRK, p. 359.

[24] Ibid, p. 380.

[25] Ibid., p. 363.

[26] Ibid., p. 381.

FOOTNOTES

CHAPTER IX

[1] Macintosh, D.C. "Toward a New Untraditional Orthodoxy." Contemporary American Theology, vol. I, Vergilius Ferm, ed. (New York: Round Table Press) 1932, p. 302.

[2] While I shall not present a Who's Who of the other contributors apart from the text, a footnote of identities seems in order here:

> George Thomas, then a member of the philosophy department at Dartmouth College became Chairman of that department at the University of North Carolina and later joined the theological faculty at Princeton.
>
> Vergilius Ferm was Professor of Philosophy and Religion at Wooster College and published in both fields. He became editor of the biographical series on Contemporary American Theology, along with Religion in the Twentieth Century.
>
> J.S. Bixler was a Professor of Theology at Harvard who became distinguished President of Colby College. He gave the Terry Lectures in Religion at Yale in 1942 which Macintosh, though stricken, was enabled to attend.

[3] Thomas, George, "A Reasoned Faith," The Nature of Religious Experience (Bixler, Calhoun & Niebuhr, eds), New York: Harper & Row, 1937, pp. 44-67.

[4] Macintosh, D.C., "Empirical Theology and Some of Its Misunderstanders," Review of Religion, May, 1939, p. 389-394.

[5] Ibid., p. 394.

[6]Ibid., p. 392.

[7]"Theology, Valuational and Existential," Review of Religion, November 1939, pp. 25-26, 27. Cf. also p. 391 of May Review.

[8]"Is Theology Reducible to Mythology," Review of Religion, January 1940, pp. 144-151.

[9]Bixler, J.S., Calhoun, R.L., ad Niebuhr, H.R., The Nature of Religious Experience (New York: Harper & Row), 1937 p. x of "Foreward."

[10]"Empirical Theology and Some of Its Misunderstanders," Review of Religion, May 1939, p. 388.

[11]Ibid., pp. 395-397.

[12]"Representative Pragmatism," Mind, vol. XXI (April, 1912), pp. 167-181.

[13]"Is 'Realist Epistemological Monism Inadmissible'?" Journal of Philosophy, Psychology, and Scientific Method, vol. X (1913) pp. 201-210.

[14]The Problem of Knowledge, New York: Macmillan, 1915.

[15]"Experimental Realism in Religion," Religious Realism (D.C. Macintosh, ed.) New York: Macmillan, 1931, pp. 307-409. Cf. esp. 361-68.

[16]Macintosh, D.C., The Reasonableness of Christianity, New York: C. Scribner's Sons, 1925, p. 200: Of 201.

[17]Sellars, Roy Wood, "Realism, Naturalism, and Humanism." Contemporary American Philosophy (C.P. Adams & W.P. Montague, eds.) New York: Macmillan, vol. II, p. 272.

[18] *Principles, Perspectives and Problems of Philosophy*, (New York: Pageant Press), 1970, p. 400.

[19] Sellars, Roy Wood, "Sensations as Guides to Perceiving," *Mind* LXVIII (1959), p. 269.

[20] *Journal of Philosophy*, XXXVII, No. 2, 1940, pp. 47-48.

[21] Sellars, Roy Wood, "Guided Causality, Using Reason and Free Will," *Journal of Philosophy*, vol. 54 (1957), pp. 487-93.

[22] Sellars, Roy Wood, "In What Sense Do Value Judgments and Moral Judgments Have Objective Import?" *Philosophy and Phenomenological Research*, 28 (1967), pp. 1-16.

[23] Cf. 18.

[24] Sellars wrote eight substantial essays on the Brain-Mind problem, most notable of these are "The Double Knowledge Approach to the Mind-Body Problem", *Aristotelian Social Proceedings*, n.s. 1923, pp. 55-70, and "An Analytic Approach to the Mind-Body Problem," *Philosophical Review*, vol. 47 (1938), pp. 461-487. Cf. also "Can Reformed Materialism Do Justice to Values? *Ethics* 55, pp. 28-45.

[25] "Naturalistic Humanism," *Religion in the Twentieth Century* (V. Ferm, ed.) New York: Philosophical Library, 1945, p. 423.

[26] "Accept the Universe as a Going Concern," *Religious Liberals Reply* (H.N. Wieman, ed.) Boston: Beacon Press, 1947, p. 171.

[27] *Reflections on American Philosophy from Within*, Notre Dame University Press, 1969, pp. 160-171.

[28] Macintosh, D.C., "The Fox Without a Tail" *The Humanist*, January 1930, p. 1.

[29] Ibid., p. 3.

[30] Ibid.

[31] Religious Realism, pp. 407-409.

[32] Readers Digest, March 1930, p. 52.

[33] Cf. Footnote 27.

[34] In a lecture at Bucknell University inaugurating the Roy Wood Sellars' lectureship, April 1971.

[35] Religious Realism, p. 409.

36) The Philosophy of Alfred North Whitehead (Paul Schilpp, ed.) Library of Living Philosophers, LaSalle, Illinois, vol. 3 (1947), p. 415.

[37] Boodin, John E., "Functional Realism," Presidential address to the Western Division of the American Philosophical Association, 1933. Cf. Proceedings and Address of the A.P.A.

[38] Boodin, John E., "God and the Cosmos," Religious Realism (D.C. Macintosh, ed.), pp. 484-85.

[39] Ibid., p. 486-87.

FOOTNOTES

CHAPTER X

[1] Miller, Randolph Crump, *The American Spirit in Theology*, United Church Press, Philadelphia, 1974, p. 112.

[2] Ibid., Chapter 6 (pp. 101-17).

[3] Meland, Bertrand E., Professor Emeritus of Theology, University of Chicago, after teaching previously at Central College, Missouri and Pomona College, California.

[4] Ogden, Schubert M., University Professor of Theology, Divinity School, University of Chicago, formerly Professor of Theology, Perkin School of S.M.U.

[5] Williams, Daniel Day, Roosevelt Professor of Systematic Theology, Union Theological Seminary, Columbia University, previously at Colorado College, The Chicago Theological Seminary and Federated Theological Faculty, University of Chicago. Various publications.

[6] Ogden, Schubert M. "Present Prospects of Empirical Theology," in *The Future of Empirical Theology*, p. 79-81.

[7] Ibid., p. 81.

[8] Ibid., pp. 81-82.

[9] Macintosh's four types of intuitions are distinguished soon in this chapter, e.g., 1) rational, 2) appreciative, 3) imaginal, and 4) perceptual. The first two are concerned with "axiomatic truth" and "intrinsic value." The latter two with certainty of reality as present and certitude of truth about reality that is not presented.

[10] Ogden, op. cit., p. 82.

[11] Meland, B.E., p. 290.

[12] Whitehead, Alfred North, *Process and Reality* is his *magnum opus* on this subject.

[13] Ogden, op. cit., p. 85, quote from Whitehead, *Modes of Thought*, pp. 140.

[14] Ogden, op. cit., p. 88.

[15] Meland, op. cit., p. 11.

[16] Ogden, op. cit., pp. 69-70.

[17] Ibid., p. 79.

[18] Meland, op. cit. pp. 287-88.

[19] *The Future of Empirical Theology*, p. 186.

[20] Ibid., p. 187.

[21] Ibid., p. 188.

[22] Ibid., p. 190.

[23] Ibid., p. 191.

[24] Ibid.

[25] Ibid., p. 194.

[26] McIntosh, *Religious Realism*, pp. 307-409.

[27] Haroutunian, Joseph, "Theology as Critique of Expostulation." Haroutunian was Professor of Systematic Theology at the University of Chicago Divinity School before his death in 1967. He had previously taught at Wellesley College and McCormick Theological Seminary.

[28] Loomer, Bertrand M., "Empirical Theology within Process Thought" in *The Future of Empirical Theology*. Loomer was Professor of Philosophical Theology at Berkeley Baptist Divinity

School and in Graduate Theology at Berkley. For many years he was Dean of Divinity School and Professor of Philosophy of Religion at the University of Chicago. For this specific reference see Meland, op. cit., p. 44.

[29]Warren, W. Preston, *Masaryk's Democracy* (N.C. and Geo. Allen and Unwin Presses. See p. 111). The Austrian rationale for executing or exiling all Czech leaders was as I quoted.

[30]"Toward an Untraditional Orthodox" in *Contemporary American Theology*, edited by Virgilius Ferm, vol. I, 1932, pp. 300-301.

[31]Warren, *Masaryk's Democracy*, p. 220.

INDEX

Names and Terms

Absolute love, 123, 125, 130, 153, 159, 207

Absolute mind, 31, 60ff, 68, 107, 131-33, 215

Action, 86-87, 214-15

Adjustment, Religious, (see Religious adjustment)

Agnosticism, 27, 48, 78, 98, 171, 193
    Avowed, 48
    Tacit,
    Critical, 48, 50-53

Alexander, Samuel, 111, 189

American Philosophical Association, 85

Ames, E. S., 33, 182

Angell, James Rowland, 21, 33

Animism, 98

Apocalypticism, 129, 152, 154

Apperception, 202
    Apperceptive Masses, 178

Aristotle, 85, 217

Art, 141, 183

Atheism, 109

Augustine, 41

Austen, Jane, 19

Bacon, Roger, 217

Bacon, Francis, 44, 91, 217

Bacon, B. W., 152

Bain, Alexander, 41, 49

Bainton, Rowland H., 14, 19-20, 22-24, 38-39

Bakewell, C. M., 61, 67-68, 163, 108

Balfour, Earl, 50

Baptists, 27, 29, 35, 43, 135, 137, 217, 218

Barth, Karl, 112, 115, 127, 170

Bartocci, Peter, 67

Bates, John, 31

Behaviorism, 56, 71, 83, 92, 174, 200

Being, 60, 168, 196, 204-207, 215

Bennett, C. A., 163-64

Bergson, Henri, 178, 214

Berkeley, George, 41, 45, 47, 59

Bertocci, ?, 66

Bixler, Julius Seelye, 13-15, 24, 125, 163-165, 167

Blackwoods Magazine, 30

Blavatsky, Madame, 62

Boodin, J. E., 131, 188, 214

Boston University, 66

Bowne, Borden P., 66

Brandeis, Justice, 7

Brandon College, 35, 216

Briand-Kellog Pact, 147

Brightman, Edgar S., 66, 67

Brodeur, Clarence, 16

Brown, Charles R., 21

Brunner, ?, 112, 115

Bunyan, John, 42

Burnett, ?, 57

Burrows, Judge, 3, 5

Burton, Professor ?, 33

Butler, Justice, 7

Byrd, Adm. Richard, 212

Caird, Edward, 31

Calcutta Lectures, 42, 44

Calvin, John,

Campbell, R. J., 35, 216

Causality, 90-91, 122, 205
    Immanent, 188
    Transeunt, 188
    Emergent, 188
    Agential, 179

Chelvicky, ?, 218

Chicago School, 27, 33, 73, 138, 162, 193, 194, 199

Christ, 65, 106, 122, 127, 137, 151-57, 158, 170, 184, 207

Christianity, 32, 95-96, 125, 129, 135, 151, 153, 156, 165, 184-186, 207, 210-211, 216

Clark, Charles E., 7

Clarke, William Newton, 194

Cleveland, Grover, 3

Clifford, N. K., 49

Collectivism, 98

Comenius, Johann Amos, 217, 218

Communication, 65, 144, 206

Communism
    Dictatorial, 155
    Christian, 155-156

Community, 65-66, 144, 154, 205-207, 216

"Community of Being", 206-207

Community of faith, 211, 214

Concretion, Principle of, 132

Conklin, Hope, 22-24

Conscientious objection, 3-5, 7-11, 17, 145-149

Constructionism, 81

Converging empiricisms,

Cosmic laziness, 189

Cosmology

Cotton, John, 29

Cowles, Genevieve, 150

Creative advance, 186, 188-189

Creative event in experience, 206, 213

Crime, 150

Cross, George, 32, 152

Cutting, Senator Bronson, 10

Darwin's *Origin of the Species*, 30

Davis, Jerome, 6, 18, 38

Davis, John W., 6, 7, 137, 161

Deiform, 182, 213, 214

Deity, 167-168

Democracy, 181

Deontology, 177, 181

Depth experience

Descartes, 197

Determinism, 58, 178

Devotion, 201

Dewey, John, 33, 69-76, 90, 101, 108-110, 144, 182, 208

DeWolfe, H. T., 106, 213

Dialectic

Dibelius, M., 152

Dionysius, 62

Disarmament, 145

Disvalues

Divinity
   Divine functioning, 123-124, 128, Chap. VII, 157-159, 166, 186

Doubt, 198

Douglas, Justice, 11

Douglas, ?, 50

Drake, Durant, 84, 85

Drummond's <u>Natural Law in the Spiritual World</u>, 30

Dualism
   Epistomological, 26, 53, 64, 78, 84, 85, 127, 162, 174, 177
   Metaphysical, 181
   Ontological, 163

Eckhart, Meister, 62, 112

Eclecticism, 114-116

Eddy, Mary Baker, 42, 62

Ego-centic Predicament, 82, 107

Election, 128, 159

Emotivism, 197
   Emotivist, 180

Empiricism, 49, 51, 53, 141, 164, 194, 195, 199-200, 208, 216
   Classical (British), 41, 44ff, 46, 47, 56, 59, 196, 204
   Radical, 69, 70, 111, 196, 202
   Whiteheadean, 195-199, 201
   Existentialist, 114, 196-197
   Sensory, 196
   Linguistic, 196

Enlightenment, 129

Entelechy

Epistemology, 76, 92-93, 110, 161, 170, 172, 191

Erigena, John Scotus, 42, 62

Evangelicalism, 18, 29, 119, 199, 218

Everett, Cotton Mather, 29

Everett, Elizabeth, 29

Everett, Walter G., 139

Evil
  Problem of, 31, 61, 64-65, 67, 107, 117, 126, 212, 215

Evolution, 176
  Emergent

Existentialism, 27, 114, 117, 164, 167, 171, 182-183, 193, 195-196, 202, 204, 208-210, 215, 216

Experience, 41ff, 44, 67-68, 70ff, 173-174, 195, 197-207
  Pure, 112-113
  Gross,
  Lived, 51, 53, 54, 14, 116, 209-?, 216

Experiment, Religious (see Religion, experimental)

Experimentalism, 69, 73, 90

Falsity, 60

Feedback, 86, 178, 180, 212

Fellowship, Douglas Clyde Macintosh, 20, 24, 191

Fenn, W. W., 100

Ferm, Virgilius, 164, 165, 167

Ferrer, J. E., 30

Festschrift, 14, 15, 37, 114, 161, 172, 173, 191, 217

Fictionalism, 68, 171

Fosdick, H. E., 184

Foster, G. B., 33, 99-100, 111, 137, 151, 193, 210

Fraser, Sir James, 101

Freedom of Will (conscience), 9, 53, 137, 178-179
  Free Choice, 214

Frei, Hans, 18

Functional Psychology, 33

Functionalism, 34, 35, 171

Fundamentalists, 170

Genius of the Whole, 189

Gestalt psychology, 198

Girouard, James Louis, 10-11

Glory of God, 125-126, 130

God, Aspects of, 59, 61, 66, 99, 103, 105-120, Chap. VII, 157-160, 165, 168, 170, 186, 199-201, 206-207, 212, 213
  As Father, 18, 153, 155, 157, 171

Goertz, Peter, 20

Gogarten, 112

Gomperz, 57

Grace, 122, 128, 204, 213

Green, Henry Copley, 23

Green, Thomas Hill, 31, 178

Griffin, Anthony, 10

Guyon, Madame, 62, 112

Half-religion, 168

Hand, Judge Learned, 6

Harbaugh, William S., 137

Hare, R. M., 180

Haroutunian, Joseph, 210

Harper, W. R., 33

Harrison, Benjamin, 3

Hartmann, ?, 143

Hartshorne, Charles, 119, 202

Hartshorne, Hugh, 38

Hartt, Julian, 15, 16, 18, 20, 23, 37-39

Harvard College, 32, 33, 37

Haydon, Eustace, 27, 108, 110, 182, 183, 184

Hebrews, 95

Hedonism, 141, 142

Hegel, George William Friedric, 27, 31, 34, 59-61, 69, 163, 204, 215

<u>Herald Tribune</u>, 5

Hermann, ?, 32

Hinderparts of God, 106, 213

Hobbes, Thomas, 45

Hocking, W. E., 110, 139, 212

Hoeffing, Harold, 193

Holl, Karl, 152

Holmes, Justice, 7, 9

Holt, Edwin B., 83

Holy, numinous, 174, 194, 198-99
    <u>Mysterium Tremendums</u>, 122, 194

Hook, Sidney, 76

House, Colonel, 147

Howison, George Holmes, 67

Hughes, Chief Justice Charles Evans, 7, 9

Humanism, 92, 96, 100, 111, 158, 182-186

Hume, David, 41, 46, 47

Huss, John, 217-218

Husserl's Essences, 14

Huxley, ?, 14

Idea(s), 45ff, 47, 67, 75, 76, 77, 80, 99, 121

Idealism, 27, Chap. III, 69, 71, 72, 84, 163, 193
   Philosophical, 54, 81, 107, 111, 192
      moral, 151
        subjective, 46ff, 48, 54, 55, 59, 60, 68, 98
        objective, 55ff, 58, 60, 68, 98
   Absolute, 33, 55ff, 59, 61, 63, 98, 163
      rationalist, 31, 32, 35, 42, 55
      voluntarist, 61, 63-64
      superrational, 61

Ideals -- Absolute, Chap. III, 137, 145, 156, 167
   Divine, 53, 109-110, 157-159, 167, 168, 186, 199

Immanence, 84, 112, 157-158

Immortality, 22, 53, 119, 125, 137, 182, 185

Impartial spectator,

Imperative, categorical

Importance, 198

Individuality, 144, 215

Ingression, 132

Instrumentalism, 35, 73, 69, 99, 196, 202

Intentionalists
   Intentionality, 202

Interpretation, Spirit of, 65

Interpreter, 65

Intuition, 116, 130, 141-142, 173-174, 177, 180, 199-200, 203
   Rational, 166
   Appreciative (aesthetic), 138, 173-174
   Imaginal, 123, 130
   Perceptual (perception-in-a-complex), 87, 118-119, 124, 165, 173-174, 177, 195, 197-198, 202, 203, 208, 212

Irrationalism, 115, 164, 170

Isaiah, Social Message of, 152

James, William, 26, 32, 33, 46, 48, 49ff, 69-75, 99, 100, 124, 202, 204, 206

Jesus, Divine values of, 106-107, 129, 151, 213

"Job", 126

Joseph, 64

Joshua, 42, 55

Journal of Philosophy, 74, 85

Journal of Religion, 173

Judgement, 77-79, 117, 204

Justified Endorsements

Kant, Immanuel, 31, 51-54, 55, 63, 67, 93, 127, 141, 142, 156, 167, 171, 181

Keane, Paul, 16

Kierkegaard, Soren, 115, 183

Kingdom of God
  as an earthly ideal, 111, 122, 129, 138, 144, 152-156, 168
  democratic, 154

Kinship of Macintosh and Sellars, 26, 175-189

Klein, David, 185

Knowing, 75, 207
  Implicative, 178
  Perceptual, 81-89, 92, 112, 176-178, 192, 195, 197-198, 202
  Mediate, 178
  Levels of, 92

Knowledge
  The Problem, 50, 76, 80, 89-90
  Theory of, 51ff, 54, 79, 119-120, 123, 140-141, 168, 176, 198, 209

Krishnan, Rada, 112

Lake, Kirsopp, 168, 169

Laotze, 62

Law, Moral, 52-53, 115

Lectures
  Bross
  Taylor, 121
  Gifford, 170
  Terry, 24, 37

Oxford, 178

Leibniz, Gottfried, 56, 58, 59, 71

Lincoln, Abe, 3

Literal religious conceptions, 170-171

Locke, John, 41, 45, 47, 53, 56, 86, 99

Loomer, Bertrand M., 210-211

Lotze, R. H., 66

Lovejoy, Arthur O., 26, 85

Luther, Martin, 96

MacDonald, Ramsay, 148

MacDougall, William, 85

Mach, ?, 41, 46

Magnus, Albertus, 62

Man, being-in-the-World

Manton, Judge, 6

Martyrdon, 62

Marx, Karl, 96, 140, 155

Masaryk, Thomas A., 218

Materialism, 30
    Billiardball
    Emergent, 181

Mathews, Shailer, 9, 33, 123, 181, 199

McMaster University, 30, 35-37, 216-217

McReynolds, Justice, 7

Mead, J. H., 33

Meland, Bernard E., 195, 196, 198, 199-200, 201-204, 206, 208, 210

Meliorism, 124

Mill, John Stuart, 41, 46, 90, 92

Mill, James, 41, 46

Miller, Randolph Crump, 19, 26, 192, 194

Mind-body problem, 60, 83, 87, 131, 158, 181-182

Miracles, 127-128

Mohammedanism, 96

Monism
   Critical, 26, 27, 85ff, 92-93, 112, 138, 191, 193, 208, 216-217
   Epistemological, 87, 92-93, 176, 192

Montague, W. P., 83

Moral optimism, 115, 124-125

Moral pessimism, 124

Morality, 5, 17, 38, 52, 61, 171, 180, 186

MORE, 204, 206

Morris, Raymond P., 17, 18

Moses, 42, 65, 106, 160

<u>Mysterium Tremendums</u>, 122, 194

Mysticism, 26, 41, 62-63, 98, 112-114, 118, 212

Mythical elements in religion, 15, 164, 169-171

Myths

Nativism, 97

Natorp, Paul, 57

Nature, 185-186, 188-189, 197, 206

Naturism, 98

Neo-Kantian, 31

Neo-orthodoxies, 27

Neo-Realism, 70, 111, 216

New Haven Register, 16, 17

New Realism, (see Rationalism -- New Realism)

Niebuhr, Reinhold, 14, 15, 114, 161, 164, 169-171

Niebuhr, Richard, 18, 114, 116, 164, 169, 171

Nisus, 111-112, 122, 189

Non-being, 60, 204

Northrop, F. C. S., 172

Numinous, 174, 194, 198-199

Objectification of reality, 74-75, 107, 203

Objectivism, 194, 195, 197

Occasions, actual

Ogden, Schubert M., 196-201, 203

Ontology, 181
  Ontological, 75, 184

Organicism, 176, 181, 187-189, 214-216

Original Sin, 117

Orthodoxy, 119, 137, 217

Otto, Rudolf, 194, 198

Overbeliefs, 121, 125, 209

Pacifism, 3, 6, 17, 147-149

Pain, physical, 61-62, 176, 204

Pain, psychic, 75, 204

Pantheism, 98, 163, 215

Patriotism, 4

Peirce, Charles, 69, 73

Perry, Raplph Barton, 82, 83, 138

Personalism, 66-67, 218

Personality, 123

Phenomenology, 168, 195, 202, 206, 208, 209, 212, 215, 216

Piety, 19, 27, 119, 192, 211, 212

Plato, 56, 57ff, 67, 143

Plotinus, 42, 62, 112

Pluralism, 58, 59, 66, 67, 163

Poetic, 170-171, 183

Poletti, W. Charles, 7

Ponty, Merleau, 202, 203

Pope, Liston, 161

Porter, F.C., 152

Powell, Emily, 21

Practicalism, 41, 42

Pragmatism, 27, 33, 34, 42, 43, 68, Chap. IV, 81, 84, 86, 99, 101, 108, 125, 141, 162, 193, 208

Pratt, R. B., 85

Prehensions

Problem-solving, 73-74

Process Philosophy, 27, 192, 198-199, 214

Psychology, 198, 210

Puritanism, 18, 140

Pythagoreans, 57

Rashdall, Hastings, 59

Rationalism -- Common Sense, 51, 81-82, 88, 118, 156, 175, 193, 216
   Realism, 26-27, 81, Chap. VI, 163, 195
   New-Realism, 82-84, 111, 216
   Critical Realism, 82, 84-88, 92, 111, 112, 120, 138, Chap. VIII, 157, 165, 175, 191-193, 202, 208, 216-217

    Essense Theory, 85
    Intentionalist, 85
    Direct perceptual, monistic, 85, 92-93, 112, 118, 124, 161-162, 175ff
    Functional, 143, 188
    Valuational Realism, 143

Rationality, 171

Reality, 56, 67, 68, 80, 98, 118, 121, 123, 143, 166, 168, 169, 173, 197, 203, 215

Reason, 86, 176, 211

Religion -- Elements of, Chap. VII, 136-137, 140
    Historical basis of, 97, 98, 118, 122, 126, 130, 137, 140, 151-152, 156-157, 166, 199, 201, 211
    Moral basis of, 103-105, 116, 122, 124-125, 130, 140-160, 165, 166, 186, 192, 212
    Philosophy of, 18, 27, 30, 89, 92, Chap. VI, 130, 161, 167, 172, 182ff, 191, 193, 209
        Taproots, 98, 167
        Essences, 96-97, 168
        Theories of Development, 53, 96-98, 103, 211-216
        Experimental religion, 89-90, 101-103, 106ff, 112, 115-119, 123, 164-167, 195, 200, 207, 209, 211
        Best philosophical basis, 36, Chap. II, 77, 123-124, 137-138, 159-160, 209-210
    Social basis of, 140, 151-157, 161, 200, 209

Religious adjustment, 29, 91, 102-105, 116, 122, 123, 125, 129, 130, 157, 165-167, 186, 207, 213

Religious idealism, 157

Religious realism, 111, 114, 137, 188

Renouvier, ?, 163

Revelation, 97, 112, 127-129, 141, 151, 159, 205

<u>Review of Religion</u>, 15, 164

Ribicoff, Abraham

Rigorism

Ritchie, ?, 57

Ritschlianism, 33, 34, 96, 99

Roberts, Justice, 7

Rogers, A.K., 85

Royce, Josiah, 32, 60, 64-66, 100

Russell, Bertrand, 91, 96

Salvation, 53, 159, 186

Santayana, George, 26, 85

Scepticism, 27, 30, 98, 193

Schiller, F.C.S., 73

Schleiermacher, Friedric, 194

Scholasticism

Schopenhauer, Arthur, 63ff

Science, 14, 26, 27, 49, 50, 69-70, 73, 76, 80, 82, 89, 90-93, 101-103, 114-116, 118, 123, 128, 137, 139, 165, 167, 172, 175, 178, 194, 200, 208, 210-213

Scott, E.F., 152

Self-realization, 60ff, 141

Sellars, Roy Wood, 26, 92, 84, 85, 88, 89, 141, 162, 175-183, 186-188, 191, 213

Sensory perception, 45-47, 51, 84, 86, 88-89, 174, 176-178, 195-197, 203

Sin, 117, 125, 126

Smith, G.B., 33

Smith, J.M.P., 33

Social philosophy, 143-157, 161

Socialism
   Fabian, 175, 181

Socrates, 57

Socratic

Solipsism, 48, 55, 59
   Solipsist, 47

Son of God

Sons of Thunder, 152

Spencer, Herbert, 49

Spengler, ?, 127

Spidle, Simeon, 41, 135-136

Spinoza, Benedict, 31

Spirituality, 116, 125, 130-131, 141, 142, 151, 166, 171, 174, 183, 186, 189

Stearns, Lewis F., 194

Stewart, 57

Stirner, Max, 48

Stone, Justice, 7, 9

Story, Judge, 7

Strong, ?, 70, 85

Subjectivism, 48, 70, 111, 194, 196, 202-204

Suffering -- Nature of, 61, 196, 204-207
    Constructive aspects, 204-205
    Transmutation of, 207
    Objectified, 205

Suffering servant, 126, 130

Sumner Charles, 3

Supernaturalism, 128, 157

Sutherland, Justice, 7

Swann, Judge, 6

Symbolism, 130, 169-171

Tawney, ?, 140

Tayler, ?, 112

Taylor, A. E., 57

Teleology, 138, 141, 166, 180

Ten Brocke, Professor, 32

Theresa, St., 42, 62, 113

Thacker, Thomas D., 7

Theodicy

Theologian [Macintosh as], 17, 19, 27, 117, 171, 200, 209, 210, 217

Theology -- Nature of, 119, 123, 167, 168, 171, 192
    Principal parts, 119-120
        Empirical, 19, 114, 117, 119, 157, 164, 167, 194-207
        Normative, 119, 129, 157, 159, 209
        Metaphysics, 34-35, 37, 99, 110, 120, 131-132, 157-160, 170, 206, 207, 209

Things-in-themselves, 51, 54

Thomas, George, 164-167

Tillich, Paul, 172, 210

Toulmin, S., 180

Traditionalism, 41-42, 47

Transcendence, 52, 63, 68, 76, 112, 122, 157-158, 168, 169

Trinity, 122, 157

Troeltsch, Ernst, 127-129, 134

Truth, 60, 72-80, 99, 168, 171, 173, 174, 185

Tufts, J.H., 33

Unity, 145, 149

University of Chicago, 1, 33, 35, 43, 96, 108, 195, 199-200, 216-217

Upanishads, 62

Urban, Wilbur, 172-173

Utilitarianism, 141, 181

Vaihinger, H., 171

Value -- Nature of, 96, 108, 114, 123-125, 137-139, 159, 165, 167- 168, 179-181, 183-185, 198, 202-205, 207, 209, 211, 212
    Types, 115, 122, 139-143
    Validation, 98, 141
    Judgement, 33- 34, 117, 180

VanDeVanter, Justice, 7

Vestsigian, Souren, 20

Voluntarism, 168

War, 6, 8, 17, 127, 145-149, 197, 211

Wardwell, Allan, 6, 7

Watson, John, 31

Webster, Daniel, 3

Weigle, Luther Allen, 37, 38, 91

Whately's Logic, 30

Whitehead, Alfred North, 26, 71, 97, 110, 187, 188, 195-199, 202, 203, 208, 210, 215,

Wieman, H.N., 108-110, 173, 199-202, 206, 210, 212

Will, 63-64, 128, 133, 142-143, 159, 166, 170, 174, 179, 195, 200, 201, 206, 207

"Will to Believe", 49

Williams, Daniel Day, 196, 204-207, 216

Wilson, Edmund, 25-26

Wilson, President Woodrow, 147

Windelband, 57

Wobbermin, Georg, 127, 128

Word of God, 97, 112

World Ground, 66

<u>World, New York</u>, 5

Wright, Henry B., 105

Wycliffe, 217

Yale University, 1, 5, 17, 24, 41, 43, 114, 162, 199

Zeller, 57

Zoroastrianism, 95

DATE DUE

HIGHSMITH #LO-45220